THE EARLY CHILDHOOD MENTORING CURRICULUM

A Handbook for Mentors

by

Dan Bellm
Marcy Whitebook
Patty Hnatiuk

Center for the Child Care Workforce,
A Project of the American Federation of Teachers Educational Foundation
Washington, D.C.

Distributed to the general public by CCW.

Distributed to the trade by Gryphon House, Inc.
P.O. Box 207
Beltsville, MD 20704
telephone: (800) 638-0928
e-mail: orders@ghbooks.com

Printed in the U.S.A. by Harris Lithographics, Inc.

Book design: Elaine Joe

ISBN   1-889956-00-7 (*Handbook*)
       1-889956-01-5 (*Trainer's Guide*)

Center for the Child Care Workforce,
A Project of the American Federation of Teachers
Educational Foundation
(CCW/AFTEF)
555 New Jersey Avenue, NW
Washington, DC 20001
T: 202/662-8005
F: 202/662/8006
E: ccw@aft.org
Web site: www.ccw.org

ACKNOWLEDGMENTS

The Early Childhood Mentoring Curriculum was made possible through the generous support of the Ewing Marion Kauffman Foundation and the Danforth Foundation. We would like to offer special thanks to Stacie Goffin, Steve Koon, Mike Helmer, Joy Torchia and Patty Mansur of the Kauffman Foundation, and to Wilma Wells of the Danforth Foundation, for their gracious help and guidance.

Many thanks also to the members of our Curriculum Advisory Board, who dedicated many hours to reviewing early drafts, and whose insight and expertise have strengthened this work immeasurably:

Betty Allen, Special Needs Resource Teacher, Eliot Pearson Children's School, Tufts University, Medford, Mass.

Pat Bolton, Family Child Care Provider, Westminster, Colo.

Diane Trister Dodge, President, Teaching Strategies, Inc., Washington, D.C.

Julie Olsen Edwards, Director, Early Childhood and Family Life Education Department, Cabrillo Community College, Aptos, Calif.

Nancy Johnson, Director, Child Care Works, Minneapolis, Minn.

Stephanie Johnson, Mentor Teacher, Associated Day Care Services, Boston, Mass.

Kathy Modigliani, Director, The Family Child Care Project, Center for Career Development, Wheelock College, Boston, Mass.

Peyton Nattinger, Director, California Early Childhood Mentor Program, Chabot College, Hayward, Calif.

An earlier version of The Early Childhood Mentoring Curriculum was developed for U.S. Army Child Development Services under Contract #MDA903-93-C-0250. Special thanks to Editorial Review Team members M.A. Lucas, Mary Ellen Pratt, Joy Guenther and Joe Perreault, who first helped bring this Curriculum to life.

We would also like to express our appreciation and gratitude to the many mentors, protégés and mentor program developers throughout the country whose groundbreaking efforts have contributed so much to the field of mentoring in early care and education.

The quotations from mentors which are interspersed throughout the *Handbook for Mentors* and *Trainer's Guide* are taken from *Mentoring in Early Care and Education: Refining An Emerging Career Path*, © 1994 Center for the Child Care Workforce.

TABLE OF CONTENTS

Early care and education is an extremely diverse field, with young children being taught and cared for daily in such varied settings as child care centers, schools, and family child care homes. Our intended audience for The Early Childhood Mentoring Curriculum is the entire spectrum of the child care field, and in particular, we are eager to bridge the divide that has often separated center-based child care and family child care. While we have developed the Curriculum primarily for use in formal mentoring programs, it can also be used in a variety of child care classes and workshops, whether at community colleges, child care centers, family child care associations, Head Start agencies or other training and staff development programs.

How To Use These Materials

Ideally, trainers and mentors will have at least 30 to 40 hours of training time to work together before the mentoring process begins. The training model for the Early Childhood Mentoring Curriculum consists of a five-day mentoring course outline, in ten half-day modules, for covering the eight units (see page 99 of the *Trainer's Guide*). These modules can be adapted to a variety of training schedules and situations.

The Curriculum is composed of two parts: this *Handbook for Mentors* and a *Trainer's Guide*.

The *Handbook for Mentors* is the primary text for the mentor training. It is designed not only as a resource for the trainer in covering the content areas of the eight Units, but as a handbook that the mentors will keep and use throughout their work with protégés. The *Handbook* contains:

* reading material for the trainer and the mentors on each of the eight Units;

* activities in each Unit that mentors can use, either on their own or with protégés;

* bibliographies in each Unit listing references and suggestions for further reading; and

* appendices with background information and resources.

The *Trainer's Guide* contains:

* goals and objectives for each of the eight Units in the *Handbook for Mentors*;

* suggested training activities, with handouts, for each Unit;

* a sample five-day mentoring course outline;

* a chapter on conducting effective group learning sessions; and

* a concluding chapter, with activities designed for the end of the mentor training course and the end of the mentors' work with their protégés.

INTRODUCTION TO MENTORING

The care of young children is among the most important kinds of work there are. Whether it takes place in child care centers, family child care homes or other settings, the daily work of teachers and providers makes a lasting difference for children, families and our society as a whole. Quality child care *matters*—and research has repeatedly shown that the key to quality child care is the presence of well-trained, well-supported and well-compensated caregiving adults.

But for many years, adults who care for young children have generally earned low wages and have had very few chances for professional advancement. Part of the problem is that many people still do not view early childhood education as a skilled profession. But more and more, we are seeing that we cannot really guarantee high-quality care for children until we "care for the caregivers" as well. In recent years, mentoring programs have become one of the most promising ways to make that happen.

What Is Mentoring?

A mentor, historically and traditionally defined, is an older, more experienced person who is committed to helping a younger, less experienced person become prepared for all aspects of life (Odell, 1990).

Mentoring programs offer new teachers and providers a practical and supportive way to learn and grow on the job. For experienced teachers and providers, mentoring programs create an opportunity to remain in the field and advance in their profession, and often, to earn financial rewards for sharing their skills with others.

In general, a mentor can be thought of as a guide, a tutor, a coach or a counselor. But in this *Handbook*, we will use the term "mentor" in the more specific sense of a teacher or family child care provider who is concerned not only with how children grow and learn, but with helping other adults to become more effective at their work. We will use the term "protégé" for the novice teacher or provider with whom you will be working as a mentor. (Other terms that are sometimes used in the field are "mentee," "peer" or "apprentice.")[1]

---

[1] For the sake of simplicity, we will also use feminine pronouns when discussing mentors and protégés, but we recognize that a significant number of men work in this predominantly female profession.

Mentors are skilled in their craft, creative in problem solving, able to reflect on their practice, flexible in relating to other adults, ready to learn new information about the process of teaching, and willing to take risks in order to grow. A mentor has worked in the child care field for a significant time, and has received education and training in child development, early childhood education and the teaching of other adults.

The relationship between mentors and protégés has certain basic qualities:

The mentor does not supervise the protégé, but rather coaches and guides as a peer.[2] The mentor provides support to the protégé if she falters, and encourages her along if her practice is less than it could be. The mentor is a trusted counselor who is committed to a close working relationship with the protégé, offering feedback that can move her to a higher level of competence and performance. The mentor is open to learning and growing, too, and is able to appreciate and benefit from the new perspectives that a protégé can offer.

The protégé is committed to her own growth and development, and to the mentor/protégé relationship. She is willing to learn new skills and reflect upon her practice with children. Like the mentor, she is ready to learn and grow.

Basic Assumptions and Beliefs[3]

Drawing from the experience of the many early childhood mentoring programs which have developed throughout the United States, the Early Childhood Mentoring Curriculum proceeds from a core set of assumptions and beliefs about the mentoring process:

* The growth and development of children, and of adults, in early childhood settings are vitally linked.

* Like children, most adults learn best by having practical, hands-on opportunities to apply new ideas and information to real-life situations. The mentoring process links classroom learning with personal guidance in caregiving practice.

* The first year of teaching and caregiving is a very important time for learning and

---

2 See "Differences Between Mentoring and Supervision," in Unit 2.

3 Adapted with permission from Newton et al. (1994), "Basic Assumptions and Beliefs," xi.

"I've known for a while that my self-esteem increases when I can help other teachers, so I was very excited by the opportunity to become a mentor. It's so stimulating and challenging. Sometimes your mentee might not really like getting critical feedback, but it is a special gift to learn how to be able to talk honestly with people about the work they are doing."

growth—a "bridge" between any pre-service training an adult has received, and her ongoing professional development.

* The mentoring process can help a child care program to become a better "community of learners"—a place where both children and adults are encouraged to reach their full potential.

* Our child care system as a whole must be improved in order to respond to the needs of an increasingly diverse population of children and families.

* The role of the early childhood teacher/provider, and the structure of our national child care system, will continue to change well into the twenty-first century. Mentoring programs are an excellent way to help caregivers prepare for such new professional challenges to come.

* While mentoring is only one response to the training and preparation of new teachers and providers, it has great potential for transforming the nature of early childhood caregiving practice.

Goals of Mentoring Programs

Mentoring programs can be structured in a variety of ways, depending on where participants work (for example, in centers or family child care homes); whether the mentoring takes place at the mentor's or protégé's place of work, or some combination; and whether an outside mentoring course or seminar takes place before or during the classroom practice. But although they vary in structure, mentoring programs are committed to three common goals:

* helping experienced, skilled teachers and providers to stay in early childhood classrooms and homes by providing recognition of their contribution and skills, and whenever possible, financial incentives;

* providing mentors with opportunities to develop their skills in communication, leadership and adult education; and

* creating increased opportunities for new caregivers to benefit from a field work experience, gain new knowledge, and improve their caregiving practices.

Why is Mentoring Important?

Teaching is one of the few professions in which the novice is expected to assume full responsibility from the first day on the job. (Hall, 1992).

In most professions, the challenge of the job increases over time as one acquires experience and expertise. In teaching, we've had it reversed. Typically, the most challenging situation a teacher experiences is in his or her first year. (Glickman, 1990).

* *Marcy Whitebook,* CCW; *co-founder of the California Early Childhood Mentor Program*

Recently I spent a morning observing a classroom for four-year-olds at a center in my community. At the end of a long circle time in a large group, the children moved to small groups for "work time." My attention was focused on one teacher—I'll call her Mary—who had six children in her group. She immediately captured their attention by holding up a plastic bag filled with wonderful hand puppets with velcro attachments. But for several frustrating minutes—for her and the children—Mary tried to get everyone to sit quietly so she could begin the activity, which consisted of each child selecting a puppet one by one and choosing a song to sing.

Keep in mind that these were terrific puppets. One had five monkeys attached to the glove; another had five pumpkins. The first child picked the monkey puppet and sang, "Five little monkeys jumping on the bed...." But by the time she got to the third monkey, the other children were grabbing at her puppet and at the other puppets resting by Mary's knee. They were having a very difficult time waiting for their turn, and I felt for them—I was finding it hard not to grab Mary's bag of treasures myself!

I kept waiting for Mary to pass out the other puppets, or at least to let the

"I've been a family child care provider for twenty years. By becoming a mentor, and responding to people's questions, I am realizing how much I know. The more we can help other providers to do a good job, the more we support ourselves and the community."

group share the puppet that was currently in use, but she didn't. She continued in the same manner for another ten minutes, with the children wiggling, distracted and barely engaged in the singing because they were so focused on wanting to touch the puppets. Two children tried to walk away from the activity completely. Mary repeatedly stopped the activity to remind the children of the rules, and by the end she seemed cross and exhausted.

I tell this story not to criticize Mary, but because it underscores the challenges that so many teachers face. When I was a child care teacher, I often found myself in situations that didn't seem to work—and watching Mary, I remembered my mentors Katy and Louise, who constantly helped me by offering gentle suggestions and alternatives.

Mary needed a mentor. In a conversation with her later that day, I learned that she had been teaching for a year and a half and had taken several early childhood education courses—thus meeting state standards for certification. She had never taken the lab practicum, however, because she could not afford to take time off her job to "volunteer" in the community college lab school. She was burning out fast. Her job was hard. In talking with her and observing her, it seemed clear to me that she had the potential and the desire to be a good teacher, but she needed help. She needed to observe other ways of doing the same activity, and she needed to reflect upon why the activity was so frustrating for her and the children.

As more and more teachers and providers enter the field with little or no training, the demand skyrockets for skilled mentors who can help them learn. Earlier and earlier in caregivers' careers, many are called upon to offer that assistance to their co-workers—often without any recognition, training or added compensation. Mary will soon be the senior teacher in her room—if she stays.

But we know that Mary is not likely to stay. Even though she has invested time and money into her specialized early childhood training, she receives little reward for having done so. Almost any other job she could get would pay more, and there is minimal economic reward for her continued training. An entry-level guard at the nearby federal prison needs only to be eighteen years old, and to have a high school diploma and no felony record. The starting salary for that traditionally male job is $18.54 an hour, more than three times the average salary for child care workers, and almost double the earnings of the highest-paid child care teachers, most of whom have earned a bachelor's degree and have years of child care experience. Mary earned only $6.75 an hour; five years from now, she will be exceedingly lucky to earn $10.00 an hour, and the prison guard will be earning at least $25.00.

Mentoring programs can help ease the burden for Mary and others like her by providing them with the skills they need, and by creating a viable career path that will give them incentives to stay in the classroom or family child care home. The first years of providing care are especially critical. Researchers have found that new staff and providers who are left in isolation to "sink or swim" tend to discard promising ideas and to revert to teaching as they themselves were taught. Support from a more experienced person can make all the difference.

Mentor programs also benefit experienced teachers and providers, by helping them gain the adult training skills they need to work with newly recruited colleagues. Mentor programs allow teachers and providers to advance professionally, and earn better compensation, while continuing to work directly with children. And since they carry the potential to diminish the severe problem of staff turnover in the field, they can greatly enhance the consistency and quality of the services that children and families receive each day.

WHAT MAKES A GOOD MENTOR?

Mentors are:

- excellent child care teachers/providers;
- committed to child care as a profession;
- willing to expand their roles to include working with colleagues newly entering or advancing in the field;
- active and open learners who are willing to participate in training sessions to enhance their mentoring and teaching skills;
- thoughtful about their own teaching and growth;
- open to differences in culture, language, personal background, and teaching and learning style among colleagues and protégés;
- sensitive and responsive to the ideas of others;
- good problem solvers (for example, can identify a problem, generate alternative solutions, choose the most appropriate solution, implement that solution, and evaluate its effectiveness);
- skilled in planning, organizing and managing work;
- familiar with the organizational structure, and policies and procedures, of their child care setting;
- aware of resources available in the community; and
- knowledgeable about the community of families and children served by the program.

Mentors have:

- a desire to become mentors and to make their mentoring relationship work;
- high expectations of themselves and the profession;
- good communication skills;
- a wide variety of teaching and caregiving skills, and knowledge of the curriculum and content of teaching;
- an interest in adults' as well as children's development;
- high integrity; and
- a sense of humor.

Mentors can:

- engage in close, supportive working relationships;
- model excellent caregiving practices;
- act as catalysts for change;
- adapt to different protégé needs and learning styles;
- resolve conflicts; and
- enlist the partnership of their colleagues in supporting new teachers/providers.

Adapted with permission from Newton et al. (1994), "Qualities, Skills and Abilities of Mentors," 2-13.

Questions for Reflection, Journal Writing and Discussion

As a tool for professional growth, we recommend that you keep a journal of your experiences as a mentor, and that your protégé also keep a journal of her classroom or family child care experiences. Journal entries can be very brief—as simple as a passing thought, an anecdote, a question, or something that your protégé has said, or as lengthy as needed to get a complex idea down on paper. Journals are discussed in more detail in Unit 3, in the section on "Reflective Practice," as an aid to reflection and dialogue between mentors and protégés.

As you begin your work with a protégé, reflect on any or all of the following questions, or write about them in your journal. Question 6 is a discussion topic that you can try with your protégé, and/or ask her to write about in her journal.

1. Has anyone ever been a mentor to you (in a child care or other situation)? Consider parents and other family members, friends, co-workers at current or previous jobs, and others in the community who have served as role models.

   ➔ What was the mentoring experience like?

   ➔ What did you most appreciate from that person?

   ➔ What did you learn?

   ✳

2. Have you ever been a mentor before (either in a child care situation or elsewhere)?

   ➔ What did you do with or for another person?

   ➔ In what ways did you feel helpful or effective?

   ➔ In what ways might you like to become more helpful and effective as a mentor?

   ✳

3. What are the three most difficult challenges a new teacher or provider faces?

  ➤ What do new teachers or providers need to learn in order to do their jobs better?

  ➤ Did you receive help in these areas during your own first year in the field?

  ➤ What was it like to begin your first job as a teacher or provider?

  ✳

4. What is your response to the story about Mary and her activity with the puppets?

  ➤ Have you had similarly frustrating experiences yourself?

  ➤ If you were Mary's mentor, what would you say or do?

  ✳

5. What are your own goals for becoming a mentor?

  ➤ What are your three greatest strengths as a teacher or provider?

  ➤ Name three areas in which you need or want to learn more in order to do your job better.

  ✳

6. For your protégé: What are your three greatest challenges on the job?

  ➤ What do you need to learn in order to do your job better?

  ➤ Name your three greatest strengths as a teacher/provider.

  ➤ Name three areas in which you'd like to improve and learn.

Glickman, C.D. (1990). "Preface." *In Mentoring: Developing Successful Teachers*, Bey and Holmes, eds. Reston, VA: Association of Teacher Educators.

Hall, G.E. (1992). "Induction: The Missing Link." *Journal of Teacher Education*, 33(3), 53-55.

Huling-Austin, L. (1990). "Teacher Induction Programs and Internships." In *Handbook on Research in Teacher Education*, W.R. Houston, ed. New York: Macmillan.

Newton, A., Bergstrom, K., Brennan, N., Dunne, K., Gilbert, C., Ibarguen, N., Perez-Selles, M., and Thomas, E. (1994). *Mentoring: A Resource and Training Guide for Educators*. Andover, MA: The Regional Laboratory for Educational Improvement of the Northeast and Islands.

Odell, S.J. (1990). *Mentor Teacher Programs*. Washington, D.C.: National Education Association.

Whitebook, M., Hnatiuk, P. and Bellm, D. (1994). *Mentoring in Early Care and Education: Refining an Emerging Career Path*. Washington, DC: Center for the Child Care Workforce.

BECOMING A MENTOR: OPTIONS AND OPPORTUNITIES

There are many different types of early childhood mentoring programs now operating across the United States. Some work exclusively with family child care providers or center-based teachers, and others work with a combination of the two.

Most mentoring programs arrange for individual mentors to work one-on-one with protégés on any and all aspects of their caregiving work, while some are oriented to completing a certain training or certificate process—for example, a Child Development Associate (CDA) credential. In some programs, mentors function as *subject matter experts* on certain topics, such as curriculum development or small business management. In still others, the entire staff of a center or family child care home serve as *model program mentors* for colleagues from a similar kind of facility, offering them general assistance in improving the quality of their program, or helping them achieve a particular goal such as accreditation.

The *setting* in which the mentoring process occurs can vary depending on the needs of the participants. Sometimes mentors and protégés meet in the mentor's home or classroom, and at other times in the protégé's. The *administration* of mentoring programs also varies; they can be managed by community colleges, child care resource and referral agencies, family child care support networks, or other training institutions or community agencies.[1]

But whatever its approach, the success of a mentoring program lies in its ability to foster strong peer relationships. A mentoring program should have a formal structure which allows mentors and protégés adequate opportunities to meet, reflect on their practices, observe each other's programs, and chart goals for change and growth. This program structure should include an assurance of:

* release time,

* classroom or family child care home coverage by qualified substitutes, and, whenever possible,

* stipends and wage increases.[2]

---

[1] For more information, see Breunig and Bellm (1996), a detailed survey of nineteen mentoring programs in the United States.

[2] In family child care, the question of earning increased compensation is generally more complicated, since most providers are self-employed managers of small businesses rather than employees. Providers, therefore, will often need mentoring on ways to enhance their child care income—including knowledge of good business practices, local regulations, and child care costs and marketing trends in the community.

Mentoring programs from across the country have now joined together in a nationwide *Early Childhood Mentoring Alliance*, co-ordinated by the Center for the Child Care Workforce (CCW), for the purposes of sharing information and resources with each other. Contact CCW for more information about the Mentoring Alliance.

Changes in the Job Descriptions and Professional Roles of Mentors

As a mentor teacher or provider, you are truly assuming a new professional role, and it takes good training and preparation to do it well. For this reason, mentoring programs work most effectively when they provide ongoing training, role models and—perhaps most importantly—support groups or other peer support mechanisms in which mentors can assist and learn from *each other*.

Although you have been selected as a mentor because of the excellence of your caregiving skills with children, it can't be assumed that these skills transfer automatically to being able to work effectively as a mentor for other adults. Mentor training, therefore, focuses primarily on the particular needs of *adult* learners and the skills needed in working with them.

Most mentors continue in their current jobs with the same group of children and co-workers, but your responsibilities and duties are likely to change as you engage in a variety of new roles with other adults. These changes should be clearly defined to co-workers and parents, with the help of your mentoring program coordinator, and release time and other scheduling issues should be carefully planned for. Co-workers may feel concerned about program coverage, or fearful about an increase in their workload. Parents may worry that their children will lose out in some way when you are engaged in other duties. In family child care programs, it will be critical to communicate with client families about your new mentoring role and how it will affect and enhance the care you offer.

Co-workers and parents can welcome these changes if they are informed about the benefits of the mentoring program and how coverage issues and other responsibilities will be handled. But as a mentor, you may need support and assistance from supervisors, mentor program coordinators or peers in demonstrating the value of mentoring, and in asking for what you need.

*"When I became a mentor, I had a chance to
help others learn about small-business skills, and they helped me learn more
about running a family day care. Knowing other providers and getting a
chance to talk about what we do makes us feel much less isolated, and that's
a big step towards improving the quality of care."*

Over the first few months, opportunities to reflect on any changes brought by the mentoring program should be a regular part of center staff meetings, or in family child care, communication with client families. Try to have realistic expectations, since no new system works perfectly at first. But many small problems can be prevented from mushrooming into large ones if they are addressed early. The assessment can be simple, focusing on:

* What's working well for the individuals involved in mentoring? Are they building the skills necessary to be effective adult trainers?

* How are the new roles positively affecting others on the team, as well as parents and children?

* What's difficult about the new set-up for the mentors, protégés, other staff, parents and children?

* What changes are needed to overcome these difficulties?

Mentoring program coordinators should be sure that everyone affected by the intro-duction of mentoring roles has an opportunity to share their views of the benefits and problems associated with the change.

Roles and Responsibilities of Participants in a Mentoring Program[3]

Mentors adopt a multitude of roles in their relationships with protégés. As you work to build a trusting relationship with a new teacher or provider, you will undertake a variety of activities. Among these might be:

* sharing information with the protégé about program procedures, guidelines and expectations;

* linking the protégé to appropriate resources;

* sharing teaching strategies or information about early childhood caregiving;

* offering support by listening and by sharing your own experiences;

* giving guidance and ideas about discipline, scheduling, planning, organizing the day, and other topics;

---

[3] Adapted with permission from Newton et al. (1994), "What Are the Roles and Responsibilities of Participants in a Mentoring Program?," 2-19 to 2-22.

* assisting the protégé in arranging, organizing and/or analyzing the physical setting of the child care center classroom or family child care home;

* counseling the protégé when difficulties arise;

* allowing the protégé to observe you or your colleagues at work and then to discuss what was observed;

* promoting self-observation and analysis;

* encouraging the protégé to reflect on her own career goals; and

* modeling professionalism (such as good working relationships with peers, and continuing professional development).

Protégés, as participants in this relationship, also have a set of roles and responsibilities to fulfill. First, they are learners—ready to hone their craft in the child care setting, to develop their own caregiving styles, and to enhance children's learning and growth. Like you, they are teachers or providers who bring knowledge of new caregiving practices to their colleagues. Protégés are responsible for working with you and other colleagues to successfully complete

a positive, first-year experience in child care work. To achieve this, they will:

* be willing to assess their own learning needs;

* participate in training sessions, professional dialogues and/or seminars on a variety of topics related to those needs;

* be active listeners and learners, identifying what they need and setting out to obtain it;

* learn from coaching and counseling from mentors and colleagues;

* observe you and other colleagues on the job when possible, and expand their variety of caregiving practices; and

* learn how to more effectively meet the needs of all the children in their care.

The Differences Between Mentoring and Supervision

A mentoring relationship is founded on peer support. Mentors are guides and role models who talk openly and directly with protégés about their work, help them improve their skills in working with children and families, and provide information and

"Becoming a mentor is another step in learning from each other. There is so little respect for this field, that we don't recognize what we know or have to offer. The Mentor Program has changed that— there is a new sense of professionalism and respect. I hope it will be realized by more and more people."

feedback. Mentors encourage protégés to take risks and meet new challenges, and help them develop their own professional goals. Mentors are open to learning, too—gaining insight from their protégés, attaining new skills, and reflecting on their own practices. Mentors do not function as supervisors, and do not conduct formal evaluations of their protégés.

While supervisors can and should use mentoring principles to help employees do the best job possible, a supervisor also has roles and responsibilities that interfere with a purely mentoring relationship—namely, the authority to fire, promote, and make other decisions about a person's job status and livelihood. Mentors often do some assessment and evaluation of protégés, but not in a way that is linked to the protégé's continued employment.

Your primary role as a mentor will be to provide support and encouragement so that your protégé has someone to rely on and turn to. A new teacher or provider is unlikely to reveal very much about herself if she is being evaluated in a way that could influence her future employment. Trust is essential for a close relationship—along with a willingness by both partners to reveal themselves and to risk making mistakes. No questions should be considered too "stupid" or too basic to ask.

Confidentiality is also an essential part of the relationship. Frankness and trust are only likely to develop when both partners know that the content of their discussions will not be shared with others—particularly with anyone who has authority over their employment status. There is an important exception, however, to this policy. If a mentor (or protégé) comes to suspect that her partner's actions or practices may jeopardize the safety and well-being of children, she has an obligation to report these suspicions to the proper authority. Child abuse reporting laws have been enacted in all fifty states precisely so that such harmful actions and practices are *not* kept secret. But in all other cases, you and your protégé should feel that you can share with each other, without worry, any doubts, questions and vulnerabilities you may have about your child care work.

Selecting Mentors and Assigning Protégés

Mentoring programs vary in the way they match mentors and protégés with each other.

Some create a detailed application and screening process in which mentors and protégés are interviewed, accepted into the program, and assigned by a mentoring program coordinator or advisory committee. Some create a self-selection process in which mentors can choose the protégés with whom they will work.

But experience has shown that several factors should be observed in assigning mentors to protégés in order to ensure effective relationships (Newton et al., 1994). Key considerations in assigning mentors include age, gender, culture, race, language, teaching and learning style, the age group of children that the mentor and protégé work with,

the content area(s) the protégé would like to focus on, and proximity of location. Again, the process should allow for the maximum level of trust and comfort to develop between mentors and protégés.

There should also be procedures to enable re-assignments when necessary. Occasionally, a mentoring relationship will not work for either or both members of a team. Mentoring program coordinators, supervisors or center directors can help you in such situations to determine whether the relationship can be improved or changed. As a mentor, you should also be free to make your feelings and opinions heard whenever a match does not seem to be working.

The process of building a strong working relationship with your protégé is discussed in greater detail in Unit 5.

Getting Started: Being a Visitor/Being a Host

You and your protégé should each think about what your expectations, fears or worries might be about visiting the other person's classroom or home for the first time, or having that person visit yours.

For example, do you fear that you will have to be "perfect" in every way? Does the protégé worry that she will be judged too harshly, or that "mistakes" she makes will be reported to a supervisor or someone else?

Share your concerns, and together make suggestions for ways to put each other at ease as a visitor or host. Talk about the differences between mentoring and supervising (as discussed in this unit), and assure each other that your discussions and observations will be kept confidential.

Breunig, G.S. and Bellm, D. (1996). *Early Childhood Mentoring Programs: A Survey of Community Initiatives*. Washington, DC: Center for the Child Care Workforce.

Caruso, J., and Foster, M. (1986). *Supervision in Early Childhood Education: A Developmental Perspective*. New York: Teachers College Press.

Ganser, T. (1991). "Beginning Teachers' and Mentors' Perceptions of Effective Mentoring Programs." Paper presented at the meeting of the Association of Teacher Educators, New Orleans, LA. ERIC Document Reproduction Service: No. ED 337-428.

Hofsess, D. (1990). "The Power of Mentoring: A Moving Force in Staff Development." *Journal of Staff Development* 11 (2): 20-24.

Huling-Austin, L. (1990). "Teacher Induction Programs and Internships." In W. R. Houston, ed., *Handbook of Research on Teacher Education*. New York: Macmillan.

Newton, A., Bergstrom, K., Brennan, N., Dunne, K., Gilbert, C., Ibarguen, N., Perez-Selles, M., and Thomas, E. (1994). *Mentoring: A Resource and Training Guide for Educators*. Andover, MA: The Regional Laboratory for Educational Improvement of the Northeast and Islands.

Whitebook, M., and Sakai, L. (1995). *The Potential of Mentoring: An Assessment of the California Early Childhood Mentor Program*. Washington, DC: Center for the Child Care Workforce.

BUILDING THE FOUNDATION FOR MENTORING: KEY AREAS OF KNOWLEDGE

As a mentor, you will be called upon to give support to others in many ways. Your protégé relies on you for what you know. How you share that knowledge and support helps your protégé to grow, and it helps you to grow at the same time. The protégé gains new information and tries to improve her work with your help. You gain new insights on how to work with others.

To serve as a mentor for a less experienced teacher or provider, you will naturally need a sound knowledge of the principles of child development and of good early childhood education practices. But in addition, there are five key areas that are critical to understand in order to be successful as a mentor:

* adult development and adult learning styles,

* reflective practice,

* respect for diversity,

* the process of change, and

* leadership and advocacy.

This Unit provides information about each of these areas of knowledge, except for leadership and advocacy, which are discussed in Unit 7.

Adult Development

As a teacher or provider caring for young children, you have come to realize how children grow and develop, how they are all unique individuals, and how professionals can guide them in positive directions along the way. Children continue to grow and develop well beyond the early years. In fact, they never stop developing—it is a life-long process.

As adults, we experience stages and/or phases of development. There are a number of prominent thinkers who, after years of research and study, have proposed various theories about how adults grow and develop.

Phase theorists suggest that there are major life tasks to be completed by each person as he or she grows. These tasks are usually accompanied by conflicts that have to be resolved at certain points in our lives. **Erik Erikson**, for example, suggests that *young adulthood* is a time when the primary conflict is between making close friends with others vs. being "on one's own" or becoming independent. Erikson's theory also includes the *maturity phase* (mid-life) when the conflict we may face is between focusing on our own accomplishments vs. sharing our knowledge and expertise with others, usually younger people (known as "generativity"). And in *old age* (later-life) Erikson believes the dominant conflict to be between integrity or pride in one's life achievements, versus despair about getting older and losing one's physical abilities.

Each of these major phases, according to the theory, may last for years. They chart a course in which successful resolution of conflict results in a new capacity to interact with what life has to offer. The resolution of young adulthood's conflict about being on one's own vs. becoming close with others, for example, results in the capacity to love. Resolution in mid-life of sharing vs. self-absorption is the capacity to care. And resolution of integrity vs. despair in later life can lead to wisdom.

The **stage theorists** describe development as a natural process of alternating periods that include balance, transitions, and a return to balance with some new level of knowledge, ability or understanding. In the theories of

Carol Gilligan, which distinguish women's stages of adult development, there are three levels:

* Level one (the early stage) suggests that an individual's primary concern is for her own well-being.

* In level two (the middle stage) the individual seeks goodness through caring for others, and values self-sacrifice as the highest virtue. This stage may be seen in many of us who work in early care and education.

* By level three, the individual has recognized herself as a legitimate person, or object of care. This suggests that she too is deserving of respect and caring, that giving all to others is not necessarily the only way to live a full life. This recognition brings about balance again and propels the adult into moral maturity, which involves the ability to see the world in at least two ways: those of caring for oneself *and* of caring for others.

These two theorists, Erikson and Gilligan, have put forward some of the most influential thinking about adult development. Despite considerable differences in their views,

"I had been teaching for thirteen years and felt it was time to leave the classroom. Part of it was the money, but I also felt I was losing my enthusiasm for the work. Then the Mentor Program came around and I decided to stay and give it a try. I realized that I was ready to teach adults as well as children, and the Mentor Program has opened up this whole new area for me. It has made me recommit to being a classroom teacher—not just for the children, but for the teachers. All of us mentors are working now to establish the role of mentor in our state certification system, to formalize the role so that long-term teachers can have a goal to move toward."

however, stage and phase theorists both believe that:

* development is an ongoing process, all our lives;

* there is a definite pattern and sequence to development;

* each stage or phase offers a different frame of reference through which individuals interact with the world;

* growth occurs through interaction between oneself, others and the environment;

* individuals play an active role in determining the course and content of their growth, and are naturally inclined to grow.[1]

Adult Learning Styles

Understanding how adults grow is central to being a mentor and working with other adults effectively in an early childhood setting. Mentors are teachers of young children and of other adults. It is important to remember that just as teachers have different teaching styles, adults have different learning styles.

Having lived more years in the world, adults bring to the learning process a complex web of experience, knowledge, skills and mindsets regarding themselves, the teacher and the topic at hand. This includes such things as their learning styles, childhood experiences (family of origin issues), cultural influences, and their own developmental stages. Many come with unexamined values and a lack of self-awareness, while others have a strong sense of identity and are quite articulate about it. Some are new to their work with children, and others have been at it a long time. In training teachers we need to discover who they are and what they bring to the learning setting. (Carter and Curtis, 1994).

As adults we bring years of experience, knowledge and skills to our learning. We

---

[1] Adapted with permission from Newton et al. (1994), "What Do the Theorists Say About Adult Development?," 1-3.

each have particular characteristics or traits that help equip us to learn in our own unique ways. Our learning styles are influenced by our childhood experiences, our families of origin, the cultures in which we were raised, our earlier schooling, and our social and economic backgrounds. Our relations to power and authority figures, and whether we are female or male, also contribute to who we are as adult learners.

Malcolm Knowles, an authority on the study of adult learning, has characterized adult learners as:

* increasingly self-directed;

* rich resources for their own learning;

* motivated to learn by the needs and interests stemming from their social roles;

* interested in learning that can be immediately applied; and

* problem-centered in their orientation to learning.[2]

In addition to a variety of learning styles and cognitive stages, other ways of knowing apply to adult learners. The theorist Howard Gardner describes *kinds of intelligence*.[3] He outlines the kind of education most of us have experienced, one which uses and values only verbal/linguistic and logical/mathematical learning. Gardner describes the many other kinds of intelligence which people bring to learning settings and, though we sometimes hear reference to them regarding children's needs, these ways of learning or knowing are rarely acknowledged in efforts to educate adults.

Intrapersonal intelligence. Learners come to understand things through individual projects, research and reflection.

Interpersonal intelligence. Social-minded people learn best when they collaborate with others to answer questions, solve problems and create representations of their understandings.

Musical intelligence. Rhythm and musical patterns are a means for these learners to develop understandings on most subjects.

Spatial intelligence. In putting together their understandings of the world, these learners do best by manipulating diverse media.

---

2 Adapted with permission from Newton et al. (1994), "What Are the Characteristics of Adult Learners?," 1-17.

3 Reprinted with permission from Carter and Curtis (1994), "Context for Adult Learning." See also Gardner (1985).

Kinesthetic intelligence. Moving around, touching and dramatizing are often a means for these learners to translate the understandings their bodies develop into more traditional models such as reading and writing.

Given the variety of learning styles and the varying stages or phases of adult development, it is important to recognize and mutually respect who each person is in a mentor/protégé relationship. Knowing about this variety of learning styles can remind us that there are unlimited ways to work together.

Reflective Practice

The ability to reflect, and to take action based on that reflection, is a significant aspect of being human. Acting upon our reflections signifies taking risks—inviting ourselves to stretch past the "comfort zone" within which most adults prefer to operate. It is when we stretch *from within* that we truly change and grow.

The effort to incorporate reflection into one's daily life is called *reflective practice*. Reflection involves thinking about and examining the experiences, activities, human interactions and events that form the fiber of our lives. We do it daily, often unconsciously, and frequently in stolen moments of solitude. Sometimes we reflect with family and friends or colleagues, but often we ponder our thoughts alone.

Reflective practice in early care and education applies a structure and sets aside the time for you as mentors and protégés to engage in conferences together, to conduct observations of one another, and to set agreed-upon goals.

Effective teachers and providers need to be able to think about their classroom/home experiences with young children, and simultaneously adjust their practices to best fit the need of the moment. This may mean altering a planned activity in favor of an unforeseen learning opportunity (what educators often call a "teachable moment"). It could mean jumping ahead to a later part of the activity or unit because the children are ready to progress more rapidly. This ability to "think on your feet" is enhanced by *reflective practice*—the ability to reflect on your own, and/or in interaction with others.[4]

Keep in mind that new protégés might not

---

4 Adapted with permission from Newton et al. (1994), "What is Reflective Practice?," 1-19.

always be accustomed to this kind of self-awareness. Your task, therefore, is to cultivate a sense of trust through close and open communication, and to gently instill an openness to reflecting on your own activities and practices in the child care program.

Reflective practice occurs as you and your protégé examine your relationship to the curriculum, the children, the parents, and your colleagues. When you become a "reflective practitioner," you can:

* identify new ways of doing daily routines and activities;

* gain better understandings about how and why you do what you do in the center or home;

* realize the need to ask for help when you are uncertain about how to handle a concern;

* plan strategies for improvements together and set goals to achieve them; and

* recognize accomplishments and repeat what works best.

One tried and true method for engaging in reflective practice in early childhood settings is as follows:

Step 1. The mentor and protégé meet to share information, discuss their work, and/or their vision for a high-quality classroom or home environment.

Step 2. The protégé identifies areas of her practice that need to be observed by the mentor: for example, handling transition times, large group activities, circle time, etc. They set a time for the observation, and the mentor asks what the protégé would like her to look for. They agree upon a tool to use or key questions to address.

Step 3. The observation is conducted. The mentor might also end the observation with a brief expression of appreciation to the protégé—for example, "Thanks for letting me observe. You looked so happy when the group was singing together. See you next week." Without this, the protégé could be left with no idea of what the mentor thinks until they meet again, and this intervening time could be agonizing.

Step 4. The protégé and mentor meet again within a week of the observation. They reflect on the observation, and the mentor asks questions of the protégé and gives feedback (describing what she saw and/or didn't see). This is called a *reflective conference*.

"Reflecting back to when I started in this field in 1985, I remember trying really hard to do my job well. I didn't have anyone from my background or culture who could be a role model I could follow. I struggled not only with the language but with the inexperience, and I didn't have an educational background. I was afraid of what people thought of me. I never asked any questions during or after any workshops or classes. It wasn't until a few years ago that I realized that I caught on to new ideas faster and easier by watching others and not by reading books."

Step 5. During the reflective conference, the mentor and protégé determine some goals for the coming period of time, and set another observation date. This time they may identify new areas to observe that relate to the new goals set.

Step 6. A second observation takes place, and the cycle is repeated.

This reflection cycle may continue, based on the needs of the mentor and protégé. Program coordinators and employers can support mentoring and make reflective conferencing a priority by providing release time or paid meeting time during work hours, and by providing coverage for mentors to conduct observations.

Unit 6 of this *Handbook* discusses in more detail the pre- and post-observation techniques that you can use to coach a protégé in reflective conferences.

Keeping a journal can be another excellent way for you and your protégé to deepen your abilities to reflect on your work. It is important to clarify with your protégé, however, that journal writing is not intended to

be an evaluation tool. Rather, it is a vehicle to encourage dialogue. We recommend that you keep a journal of your mentoring experience, and that you ask your protégé to keep a journal as well.

You should not assume, however, that all adults will embrace the opportunity to communicate in written form. Some may be concerned about their reading and writing skills—especially if you will be working in English, and English is not their first language. If you are going to ask your protégé to keep a journal, it will help to offer her a non-threatening definition of what a journal is and what "journal dialogues" can accomplish. Emphasize that journal entries can be very brief—they can be as simple as a passing thought, an anecdote, a question, or something a child has said, or as lengthy as needed to get a complex idea down on paper. An entry could be a reaction to something that happens in the child care program, or a response to something that someone else has written.

Before you can use your journals in dialogue, you also need to establish a significant level of trust. Two questions—Who gets to read this? and What do you do with this information?—should be addressed from the outset, since the answers may have a direct bearing on what will be written down and disclosed in the journal.

Informal times can also be productive learning opportunities for mentors and protégés to engage in reflective practices. You can:

* have a cup of coffee together before work, at lunch, or during nap time;

* agree to "drop in" when possible to look at a particular concern of your protégé;

* jot down a few comments or questions for your protégé before you go;

* visit a team meeting to plan curriculum;

* invite your protégé to visit your classroom/home and encourage her to observe you or another mentor; and

* suggest resources or other literature to read and discuss.

Reflective practice is important because it:

* enables caregiving adults to discuss issues, set goals, and change practices in a supportive climate;

Questions to Promote Reflection

→ Can you talk more about that?

→ Why do you think that happened?

→ What evidence do have about that?

→ What do you need?

→ What have you tried before?

→ Why did/didn't it work?

→ What does this remind you of?

→ What if it happened this way?

→ How else could you approach that?

→ What do you want to happen?

→ How could you do that?

→ When is the concern most pronounced?

Affirmations to Support Reflection

→ You can find a way that works for you when you are ready.

→ You can change if you want to.

→ You can grow at your own pace.

→ You can know what you need and ask for help.

→ You can experiment and explore. I will help you.

→ Your needs and reflections are important.

→ I like talking to you.

Adapted with permission from Newton et al. (1994), "Activity 1-11, Handout," 1-115.

✳ allows for professional growth in both the mentor and the protégé. You grow by learning how to foster the growth of the protégé based on mutually agreed-upon goals. Your protégé grows by learning how to develop her own classroom/home based on educational theory and best practices.

Combined with a knowledge of how adults learn and grow, and a respect for different learning styles, reflective practices are the cornerstone of what mentors and protégés do together to improve their skills, interactions, and growth as child care professionals.

Respect for Diversity in Early Childhood Settings: Culturally Relevant Anti-Bias Education

As a child care teacher or family child care provider, you are actively involved in the lives of all kinds of young children and their families every day. You know that an essential ingredient in children's ability to grow and develop well is a positive self-identity and self-esteem.

Excellent caregivers reinforce a positive sense of self among children. They appreciate children's differences and similarities in race, gender, ethnicity, creed, language, ability and class background. They encourage children to be comfortable with who they are. They help children develop critical thinking skills to resist bias. And they develop programs that reflect children's home cultures. Research, too, confirms that:

✳ Children notice differences well before the age of two. In fact, they *learn* by noticing differences.

✳ Once they notice differences, children become vulnerable to biases in the society.

✳ Adult discomfort in helping children deal with differences can make children feel uncomfortable themselves.

✳ By the age of nine, children's attitudes toward racial, ethnic and cultural differences generally become solidified and resistant to change, often requiring a major life experience to alter them. The "window of opportunity" between infancy and age nine is a critical time for teachers and providers to help children form a positive self-identity and a bias-free respect for diversity.[5]

---

5 Adapted with permission from Derman-Sparks (1989).

At the same time that we are seeking to develop culturally diverse and responsive programs for children, mentors and protégés must also be active in promoting understanding and respect in their working relationships among *adults*. For all of us, becoming free of prejudice is an ongoing process of learning and practice, and each person is at a different place along the journey. Some people "internalize" the dominant culture's prejudices and stereotypes about their own group to the point where they appear to accept or agree with them. Others may deny differences altogether—saying, for example, that "We're 'color blind' in this program. We see all people as the same." This notion of "color blindness" not only rejects the reality and the value of human diversity, but is in itself a form of bias.

Louise Derman-Sparks, a noted anti-bias educator, has written about the stages which adults go through in the effort to unlearn bias:[6]

Stage 1. Awareness: learning about the patterns and sources of discrimination prevalent in our society, our culture and ourselves. We come to recognize that we have all been scarred by it.

Stage 2. Exploration: digging deeper into the root causes of prejudice; examining our own experiences and origins, and any stereotypes we may have been taught about race, class, ethnicity, sex roles and sexual preference; searching for evidence of bias in our classroom or home learning environments.

Stage 3. Inquiry: asking for more information about causes, roots and symptoms of bias, and seeking out ways of changing those negative patterns and belief systems.

Stage 4. Reflection: sharing with each other, as mentors and protégés, what we have learned, what we would like to change, and how we might go about doing so.

Stage 5. Utilization: putting into practice new approaches toward becoming freer from bias: for example, changing one's classroom/ home environment, curriculum content, and interactions with others in order to be culturally relevant and respectful of diversity.

These stages can provide you with a framework for embarking and continuing on your own journey, beginning with yourself.

---

6 Ibid.

Guiding Principles for Anti-Bias Education in Mentoring[7]

* Anti-bias education begins with caregivers and children and expands outward—to co-workers, families, the community, and beyond.

* Anti-bias education is for *everyone*, not just certain racial, ethnic or cultural groups. Understanding that *everyone* has been harmed by racism, sexism, handicappism, homophobia and class divisions means that each person has work to do to undo prejudice.

* Anti-bias education requires a sustained and integrated approach; it should become part of a program's daily practices, not just at holidays or special times of the year.

---

7 Ibid.

DEFINITIONS OF KEY CONCEPTS

Bias Any attitude, belief or feeling that results in, and helps to justify, unfair treatment of an individual because of his or her identity.

Bigotry An extreme form of prejudice, often accompanied by hostile actions, threats, intimidation, and violence.

"Isms" (Racism, Sexism, Handicappism, Classism, Homophobia, etc.) Any attitudes, actions, or institutional practices that subordinate people due to an aspect of their identity.

Prejudice An attitude, opinion or feeling formed without adequate prior knowledge, thought or reason. Prejudice can be a pre-judgment for or against any person or group.

Stereotype An oversimplified, and often negative, generalization about a particular group.

Adapted with permission from Derman-Sparks (1989).

* There is no single "recipe" for an effective anti-bias curriculum. Mentors and protégés can adapt the principles of anti-bias education to their own settings and build their own versions.

* Anti-bias education uses and builds on known early childhood practices. No new or unusual methods need to be applied.

* Building respect for diversity requires adults to examine themselves. This means that trust—and confidentiality—must be established between the mentor and protégé, as they explore their own biases and their own experiences of discrimination.

* Mentors and protégés must feel free to be forthright and honest with each other, in an atmosphere that is both supportive and challenging, as they examine themselves and their practices. This can be difficult and painful, but the resulting growth can be wonderfully satisfying.

The Process of Change

As a teacher or provider, you are actively involved each day in guiding, stimulating and encouraging growth in young children.

This makes you an "agent of change." You are fostering new learning, answering questions, acting as a role model, and demonstrating caring in all aspects of your involvement with the children.

Though at times it may be difficult to imagine, change can have a positive impact on you, your colleagues, your program and the families you serve. Change is growth—and it is central to the mentoring process. The mentor/protégé relationship is structured to offer true support to the protégé in making changes which, in turn, generate growth in you as a mentor.

Several key understandings have emerged from the work of educational researchers about change in individuals and organizations:[8]

Change is a process that takes time, not a single event.

* There are stages to change. In most cases, it doesn't "happen overnight." It takes time to plan for change, to build a mentor/protégé relationship (see Unit 5), to try new practices, and to incorporate innovations into programs effectively so that the changes will

---

[8] Adapted with permission from Newton et al. (1994), "The Change Process," 1-35 to 1-39.

last. People and systems tend to become accustomed to certain ways of doing things, and sometimes they alter slowly.

Change can be exciting—or difficult and unpleasant—or all of these at once.

* Change can be exhilarating, a relief, a catalyst for hope, and a way of building a sense of community. But even though change is a natural and inevitable part of living and working, there is often resistance to it at both the personal and organizational levels. Not everyone will feel open and receptive; some might prefer to keep old ways in place. Such conflicts are also a natural part of the process. Although change can energize and renew a group or organization—especially when all agree that it is necessary and will lead to improvements—it is realistic to expect that it will be difficult to change older practices or systems quickly.

Change is accomplished by individuals before organizations.

* Change begins with the individual. It does not come about in an organization until members of that organization embrace and "own" the change—in other words, believe that it is for the best, and understand why.

This requires dialogue and information-sharing. Change has the best chance of being successful and lasting when it is generated by the individual members of the system or organization themselves.

Change is a highly personal experience.

* People have varying perspectives on and responses to change, and each person is ultimately responsible when it comes to moving along a path of change. There is no single "right" way of accepting or appreciating change. But when each individual's progress in the change process is allowed for and understood, the change has a better chance of succeeding.

Change is best understood and accepted when it clearly defined.

* Individuals need to know what will be different as they adopt change, how long it will take, and what will be required of them. When goals and expectations are well-defined, and there is clear evidence that the proposed changes can be effective, individuals will generally feel less anxious about and more accepting of the process.

As you and your protégé seek to bring about new ways of relating to each other and to your child care settings, there will be many challenges. Learning about the change process can help you do this new work. Keep in mind that you are not only bringing about changes in your relationships with each other, but with children, families, co-workers and others in the early childhood profession. Some knowledge and understanding about how change occurs can help you to be more effective in creating successful mentoring experiences.

Activity 1: Reflective Practice

1. Ask your protégé to select an important issue or problem that arose for her in her child care program during the past week, and make a list of three ways in which the situation might be addressed.

   *

2. Ask the protégé to share this information with you, either in written form from a journal, or orally.

   *

3. Ask questions of the protégé to help her develop steps to address the issue or problem. Both of you can take notes.

   *

4. Together, set a timeline for making changes, and decide whether (and when) an observation would be helpful.

   *

5. If an observation is agreed upon, implement it. Then meet after the observation, and refine your goals and plans as needed.

   *

Note: Keep in mind that you, too, as a mentor, can benefit from having reflective conferences with a mentoring program coordinator, trainer or fellow mentor to guide you in your own work with your protégé.

Activity 2: The Diversity Wheel[9]

You and your protégé can learn more about each other, and about how our society treats human diversity, as you discuss these aspects of who you are.

1. Draw a large wheel or a pie chart and draw lines that divide it into a number of "slices." On each "slice" write some aspect of how your identity or culture is defined and shaped. Labels for "slices" could include: race, ethnicity, religion, class (economic background), age, physical ability, sexuality and gender.

*

2. Make notes in each section about how you were raised. What ways did you change as you grew older? Why?

*

3. Reflect on the following questions:

   ➤ What values were you taught about each of the areas on the "pie?" Did you agree or disagree with how you were taught? Why? Why not?

   ➤ How do you think society currently values each of your "pie slices"? Are they viewed as positive, negative, or neutral in terms of bestowing privileges, respect, status, freedom, wealth, etc.?

   ➤ How do you respond to each of your "pie slices"? Which aspects of your identity do you feel positive, uncertain, uncomfortable, and/or neutral about? How might any of these attitudes affect your mentor/protégé relationship?

   ➤ In what areas would you still like to grow and make changes? Agree with your protégé to support each other in those tasks and chart strategies to make it happen.

---

9 Adapted with permission from Bellm and Whitebook (in press).

Activity 3: Interrupting Discriminatory Behavior

1. Read "Interrupting Discriminatory Behavior" on page 49.

＊

2. Discuss: Have you ever interrupted an insulting remark or act between children and/or adults? What happened? Describe the incident.

＊

3. Discuss how you might have handled the situation differently. What was positive about your intervention? How did you know?

＊

4. If you overheard or witnessed an insult but did not intervene, why not? What would you need in order to respond differently in the future?

＊

5. Make a plan to implement the "Ten Steps" the next time you hear an insult. After you use it, describe to your mentor/protégé what happened. Make notes in your journal about the incident.

＊

6. Share strategies and feedback about how to improve your responses. Record these in your journal for reference.

Activity 4: The Process of Change

1. With your protégé, brainstorm a list of potential obstacles (both personal and organizational) you each face in becoming better teachers/providers through mentoring. What barriers are there to your having a successful mentor/protégé relationship?

*

2. Select three personal concerns and three organizational concerns, for a total of six. Review the choices you have made and prioritize the top two you wish to address.

*

3. Examine why you believe these two areas of difficulty exist. Once you both understand the reasons, consider the following questions:

   → If this barrier did not exist, how would we be more successful? What would we do?

   → What are the ways we can discuss these obstacles with others that could help overcome them? Who should we work with? How can we get more information to others?

→ What must I do to overcome my personal obstacle(s) in becoming a better mentor/protégé? How can we help each other?

→ How will the mentoring program make my job better?

→ What can we learn by overcoming these obstacles? Will we gain new skills? If so, what are they?

*

4. Prepare a strategy for addressing the two concerns that include a personal approach and an organizational approach.

*

5. Weave this activity into your ongoing discussions, and chart the progress you are making on your strategies regularly.

*

6. Once you have achieved success, take on other challenges from your lists.

*

Note: It can also be helpful for both of you to write about this process in your journals.

INTERRUPTING DISCRIMINATORY BEHAVIOR

1. **Don't ignore it.** Do not let an incident pass without remark. To do so gives the message that you are in agreement with such behavior or attitudes. If the intervention would jeopardize anyone's safety, it should not take place at the exact time or place of the incident, but it must be brought up as soon as appropriate.

2. **Explain and engage when raising issues.** Avoid preaching or being self-righteous.

3. **Don't be afraid of possible tension or conflict.** In certain situations this may be unavoidable. These are sensitive and deep-seated issues that won't change without some struggle. Try to model for children and co-workers that constructive conflict can be positive and resolved.

4. **Be aware of your own attitudes, stereotypes and expectations, and be open to discovering the limitations they place on your perspective.** We are all victims of our misconceptions to some degree, and none of us remain untouched by the discriminatory images and behaviors we have been socialized to accept.

5. **Project a feeling of understanding and forgiveness when events occur.** Don't assign guilt or blame.

6. **Recognize that you may become frustrated.** Discriminatory behavior won't be eradicated in a day or from one "multicultural presentation." Sometimes things may seem to get worse before they get better. This is a constant process of change and growth, even in a supportive environment.

7. **Be aware of your own hesitancies to intervene in these situations.** Be willing to examine your own fears about interrupting discrimination.

8. **Be a role model.** In everything you do with children and adults, reflect and practice the positive values you are tying to teach.

9. **Be non-judgmental but know the bottom line.** Issues of human dignity and equality are non-negotiable.

10. **Distinguish between categorical thinking and stereotyping.** For example, "redheads" is a category, but "redheads have fiery tempers" is a stereotype.

Adapted with permission from Guidice and Wortis (1987).

Belenky, M., et al. (1986). *Women's Ways of Knowing: The Development of Self, Voice and Mind.* New York: Basic Books.

Bellm, D. and Whitebook, M. (in press). *Leadership Empowerment Action Project (LEAP): A Training Guide for the Early Childhood Community.* Washington, DC: Center for the Child Care Workforce.

Carter, M., and Curtis, D. (1994). *Training Teachers: A Harvest of Theory and Practice.* St. Paul, MN: Redleaf Press, Inc.

Chang, H., Muckelroy, A., and Pulido-Tobiassen, D. (1996). *Looking In, Looking Out: Redefining Child Care and Early Education in a Diverse Society.* San Francisco: California Tomorrow.

Clift, R.T., Houston, W.R., and Pugach, M.C. (1990). *Encouraging Reflective Practice in Education.* New York: Teachers College Press.

Council on Interracial Books for Children, and Multicultural Project for Communication and Education. (1984). *Child Care Shapes the Future: Anti-Racist Strategies* (filmstrip). New York: CIBC.

Derman-Sparks, L., and the ABC Task Force (1989). *Anti-Bias Curriculum.* Washington, DC: National Association for the Education of Young Children.

Duff, C.S. (1993). *When Women Work Together.* Berkeley: Conari Press.

Erikson, E. (1950). *Childhood and Society.* New York: W.W. Norton.

Erikson, E. (1968). *Identity, Youth and Crisis.* New York: W.W. Norton.

Erikson, E. (1982). *The Life Cycle Completed.* New York: W.W. Norton.

Gardner, H. (1985). *Frames of Mind.* New York: Basic Books.

Gilligan, C. (1982). *In A Different Voice.* Cambridge: Harvard University Press.

Gilligan, C., Ward, J.V., and Taylor, L., with Bardige, B. (1988). *Mapping the Moral Domain.* Cambridge: Harvard University Press.

Guidice, A. and Wortis, S., eds. (1987). *Cultural Links: A Multicultural Resource Guide.* Cambridge, MA: Multicultural Project for Communication and Education (out of print).

Hidalgo, N. (1993). "Multicultural Teacher Introspection." In T. Perry and J. Fraser, eds., *Freedom's Plow*. New York: Routledge.

Kegan, R. (1982). *The Evolving Self: Problem and Process in Human Development*. Cambridge: Harvard University Press.

Kegan, R. (1994). *In Over Our Heads: The Mental Demands of Modern Life*. Cambridge: Harvard University Press.

Knowles, M. (1978). *The Adult Learner: A Neglected Species*. Second edition. Houston: Gulf Publishing Co.

Levine, S.L. (1989). *Promoting Adult Growth in Schools: The Promise of Professional Development*. Boston: Allyn and Bacon.

Levinson, D. (1978). *The Seasons of a Man's Life*. New York: Knopf.

Levinson, D., and Levinson, J. (1996). *The Seasons of a Woman's Life*. New York: Knopf.

Lieberman, A. and Miller, L., eds. (1991). *Staff Development for Education in the '90s: New Demands, New Realities, New Perspectives*. Second Edition. New York: Teachers College Press.

Newton, A., Bergstrom, K., Brennan, N., Dunne, K., Gilbert, C., Ibarguen, N., Perez-Selles, M., and Thomas, E. (1994). *Mentoring: A Resource and Training Guide for Educators*. Andover, MA: The Regional Laboratory for Educational Improvement of the Northeast and Islands.

Schon, D.A. (1990). *Educating the Reflective Practitioner*. San Francisco: Jossey-Bass.

Whitebook, M., Hnatiuk, P., and Bellm, D. (1994). *Mentoring in Early Care and Education: Refining An Emerging Career Path*. Washington, DC: Center for the Child Care Workforce.

GROWING AND DEVELOPING AS A TEACHER OR PROVIDER

People who study human development have come to believe that learning is a lifelong process that human beings enjoy. As we discussed in Unit 3, there is now much greater understanding in the field about the ways in which adult development differs from (but continues) the process of child development.

Researchers have also proposed various theories of the stages of *teacher and provider development*—the different needs, concerns and abilities that caregiving adults will have at different times in their careers. A basic understanding of these stages can help you to identify your own current level of practice, and your own priorities for learning and growth.

Stages of Teacher/Provider Development[1]

In recent decades, researchers have been studying the ways in which teachers grow from the pre-teaching level to the stage of becoming mature professionals. The accompanying chart outlines a theory of teacher development proposed by Lilian G. Katz, a leading expert in this area. Her work shows that although new and experienced teachers and providers are at different stages of growth, they are all traveling along the same basic path. Although there is some disagreement about the number of stages involved, all researchers agree that the level of complexity of learning and development increases as caregiving adults grow:

* from concern with self and survival ➡ to a more child-centered orientation;

* from insecurity ➡ to confidence in job performance;

* from the use of a small variety of teaching and caregiving strategies ➡ to an ever-expanding collection of strategies to meet the needs of the diverse children in their care;

* from a fear of change ➡ to an acceptance that change is an essential process of life;

* from concern with their own classroom/home ➡ to a wider commitment to the child care profession and a greater involvement in professional activities.

---

[1] Adapted with permission from Newton et al. (1994), "How Does Research Regarding Teacher Development Relate to Adult Development?," 1-11.

STAGES OF PRESCHOOL TEACHER DEVELOPMENT

Lilian Katz (1972)

STAGE 1. THE SURVIVAL STAGE

Mainly concerned with surviving, she realizes the discrepancy between anticipated success and classroom realities; might feel inadequate and unprepared.

STAGE 2. THE CONSOLIDATION STAGE

(second and third year of teaching)

Consolidates gains made in the first stage; begins to focus on individual children and differentiates specific skills and tasks to be mastered next.

STAGE 3. THE RENEWAL STAGE

(third and fourth year of teaching)

Might tire of doing same things and want to look for innovations in field.

STAGE 4. THE MATURITY STAGE

(three or more years of teaching)

Has come to terms with self as teacher; asks deeper and more abstract questions.

(Note: Length of time teacher spends in each category can vary greatly.)

If we look at the following testimonials given by mentors at a recent national gathering, we can see that many of them were showing signs of a mature stage of growth: a new level of self-confidence and sense of self-worth, a willingness to face risks, changes and challenges, an openness to learning from others (including new teachers) and a readiness to make a wider commitment to the child care profession:

"By becoming a mentor, and responding to people's questions, I am realizing how much I know. The more we can help other providers to do a good job, the more we support ourselves and the community."

"I needed a new challenge....I feel so much better about myself and what I can contribute."

"I've known for a while that my self-esteem increases when I can help other teachers....It's so stimulating and challenging. Sometimes your mentee might not really like getting critical feedback, but it is a special gift to learn how to be able to talk honestly with people about the work they are doing."

"The Mentor Program came at a critical point. I was ready to leave the field. I felt like the Program said to me, "You are a teacher, a professional and an advocate," and it helped me recognize that I have those skills."

"I was looking forward to having a mentee but I didn't realize what I would learn from her. My mentee was one of those people who sees the shining light in the most challenging child. It really helped me to see some of the children differently through her eyes. I have been given at least as much as I have received."

"I am a toddler teacher but I never intended to teach lower than third grade. I decided to stick with my job until I could get one in the public school. After three years I finally began to feel comfortable about what I was doing. If I'd had a mentor, if someone had helped me learn what I needed to know to care for kids at this age, it would have been so much easier and more fun. I get a lot of satisfaction as a mentor, helping others get started. My own teaching is improving as I think about what I am doing and why. Now I'm not waiting for a "real" teaching job. I am in child care, and I know I am already working in the field of education."

The Needs of Beginning Teachers and Providers

Research on caregiver development shows that new teachers and providers generally share a particular set of needs. Their most common needs might be summarized as follows:

Teaching/Caregiving Needs

* organizing play and learning activities, and planning daily, weekly or monthly curriculum units;

* building confidence in how to manage a group of young children;

* learning how to use a variety of methods, materials, strategies and techniques;

* addressing the individual needs of children through individualized caregiving approaches;

* assessing each child's development and progress;

* understanding the causes of children's behavior, and responding with effective and positive techniques of guidance and discipline;

* communicating with and relating to parents (especially in family child care, in which parents are in a more direct client role with the provider).

Emotional Needs

* overcoming feelings of isolation;

* interacting with colleagues;

* recognizing their strengths and successes as caregivers, as well as their challenges and needs for growth;

* coping with stress;

* managing time;

* preparing for and responding to evaluations from one's supervisor, or (in family child care) from a licenser or other regulatory agency.

Resource Needs

* receiving advice on resources and materials for teaching;

* obtaining materials and supplies;

* (in family child care) learning skills and information related to managing a small business; and

* gaining knowledge of training, support and other professional opportunities in the community and in the broader child care field.[2]

The Qualities of Experienced and Effective Teachers and Providers

As you support a new teacher or provider, you are enabling that person to develop effective caregiving practices. And as your protégé goes through the mentoring process, she will become more skilled at reflecting on her own practices.

A basic knowledge of the elements of excellent teaching can help you and your protégé to develop a common professional language. Then, as you work together, you will both be working toward the same goals of excellence.

Effective, excellent teachers and providers can be characterized as having a common set of qualities:

* a mind-set of continual curiosity, and a commitment to lifelong education and learning;

* reflectiveness about their own practice, and honesty in assessing their own professional skills;

* a caring for and about children as learners and people of value;

* attentiveness to and appreciation for what children do and say;

* an ability to work cooperatively with other learners;

* an appreciation of—and a commitment to understanding and addressing—children's and adults' differences in culture, ethnicity, language and learning style;

* an understanding of the developmental characteristics of the children they care for;

* an ability and commitment to work in partnership with parents to provide the best care possible;

---

2 Adapted with permission from Newton et al. (1994), "Needs of Beginning Teachers Identified in the Literature," 2-11.

"After seven years of teaching, I was at a crossroads. I didn't really want to leave my classroom, but I kept thinking about what I should do next. I needed a new challenge. Becoming a mentor teacher re-energized me—I was able to learn more about myself as a teacher, and I have learned a lot from my student. I feel so much better about myself and what I can contribute."

* an extensive collection of caregiving approaches and strategies; and

* an ability to facilitate the growth and development of others, generating a sense of purpose, joy and excitement about learning.[3]

Helping A New Teacher or Provider Move Toward Excellence[4]

The process of becoming an excellent teacher or provider is an ongoing journey. While we all achieve many milestones along the way, we never arrive at a final destination. Regardless of our number of years in the profession, we are always in the process of trying on new ideas, strategies, or ways of thinking about our work.

For a new teacher or provider, most of what she does, plans, and thinks about each day will be new. For you as a mentor, working with a protégé will provide a freshness to your own approach and add a new dimension to your practice.

Excellent care and education is a goal for all child care programs. But we must emphasize that *excellence involves risk*. If teachers and providers are to achieve excellence, they must be encouraged and supported in going through a process of trial and error—taking risks and reflecting on what worked, what didn't work, and why.

A mentoring program, therefore, must create a climate in which caregivers are allowed to test barriers and make mistakes. This is a concept that you can weave constantly into conversations with your protégé. Emphasize that when adults are part of a learning community themselves, it enhances the well-being of the children in their care. As adults become more confident and secure about their skills and abilities, they become positive models of healthy self-esteem for children.

Just as students of dance have mirrors to provide them with specific feedback about their balance and technique, all of us in the field of early care and education need "mirrors" that can reveal the quality and limitations of our practice. The reflections in the eyes of the children we care for are not enough, even though they are highly informative and useful as clues and guides. Through a variety of techniques outlined in the next two chapters, mentors can provide a clear and helpful "mirror image" to adults who are just setting out on the path toward excellence.

---

[3] Adapted with permission from Newton et al. (1994), "Effective Teaching and Beyond," 3-8.

[4] Adapted with permission from Newton et al. (1994), "Instructional Leadership," 3-15 to 3-16.

Activity 1: Stages of Development

1. Read the article "Teachers' Developmental Stages" by Lilian G. Katz (Appendix 1), and then write briefly in your journal about your own stage of development. What are the characteristics of this stage? Which developmental "hurdles" have you already passed? What are the main challenges that now lie ahead for you? Would you revise Katz's four-stage model in any way, if it does not seem to apply closely enough to your own experience?

2. Ask your protégé to do a similar self-evaluation, either in an informal discussion or in writing, using the Katz article as a resource. Are there any significant differences in the ways that you and your protégé assess the protégé's level of development? If so, what do these differences reveal? What steps do you need to take so that you and your protégé can reach agreement on your goals for the mentoring relationship?

✳

Activity 2: Questions for Reflection, Journal Writing, and Discussion

Note: This can be an activity for working with your protégé, and/or with other mentors.

1. ***Turning Points.*** Think about your journey as a teacher or provider: where you started, the various roles you have played, and how you have grown. What turning points have you faced? Reflect on those places in your journey where you came to a "fork in the road" and had to make a choice. Select one of these "turning point" experiences to think about in detail. What did you learn from the experience? Who was with you on that "road"? How did others contribute to the insights you gleaned from the experience? How has the experience left its mark on you as a teacher or provider?

✳

2. ***Peak Experiences.*** Reflect on the "peak experiences" you have had in your professional development—high points that

have particularly contributed to your growth. Select one to think about in detail. What was the experience and how did you become involved? Were others part of the experience? What role did they play? How did the experience influence your thinking about what is important in caring for young children? What insights did you gain? How have those insights influenced choices you have made since then?

*

3. **Risks.** What risks have you taken as a teacher or provider in your quest to enhance your own teaching and learning? Select one risk experience—big or small—that really paid off or taught you something important. What did you do? How did you feel? What did you learn from the experience?

*

4. **Leaders.** Think about individuals you admire as leaders—in the world, in your community, in the child care field, or in your own home or work place. They might be well known or relatively unknown. Then select one leader you particularly respect to think about in detail. Why do you respect this person so much? What special qualities does this person exhibit? How does this person affect the lives of others? How has this person shaped your beliefs about leadership, or about your own role as a leader? What do you believe are the three most important qualities a leader should possess, and why?

Jones, E. (1993). *Growing Teachers: Partnerships in Staff Development.* Washington, DC: National Association for the Education of Young Children.

Katz, L.G. (1972). "Developmental Stages of Preschool Teachers." *Elementary School Journal* 73 (1), 50-54.

Levine, S.L. (1989). *Promoting Adult Growth in Schools: The Promise of Professional Development.* Boston: Allyn and Bacon.

Newton, A., Bergstrom, K., Brennan, N., Dunne, K., Gilbert, C., Ibarguen, N., Perez-Selles, M., and Thomas, E. (1994). *Mentoring: A Resource and Training Guide for Educators.* Andover, MA: The Regional Laboratory for Educational Improvement of the Northeast and Islands.

Yonemura, M. (1986). *A Teacher At Work: Professional Development and the Early Childhood Teacher Educator.* New York: Teachers College Press.

BUILDING RELATIONSHIPS
BETWEEN MENTORS AND PROTÉGÉS

Trust is the key to a successful mentoring relationship for you and your protégé. Sometimes you can build trust with another person with little effort. But more often, trust results from careful attention to your own and your protégé's needs, and from clear expectations about each other's roles and responsibilities.

Successful mentoring also depends on good communication, which in turn calls for you to be aware of things about yourself that influence how you relate to other people. Part of your training as a mentor will involve thinking about how your individual strengths and weaknesses, and your beliefs and attitudes, help or hurt your interactions.

Learning about yourself is not a simple or one-time event. It is a process that occurs over a lifetime, and your experience as a mentor will contribute to your self-awareness. As we discussed in Unit 3, by understanding similarities and differences in how people develop, react and change, you will learn about yourself as well as your protégé. And as you practice reflection, you will build your skills in understanding and analyzing interactions between people. These skills will help you support new teachers or providers in their personal and professional growth.

Getting to Know Each Other

There are no hard and fast rules about what makes a good match between a mentor and a protégé. Mentors usually are older than protégés, and protégés typically can identify with them for some reason—for example, if they are part of the same cultural community, or have similar child care experience. These similarities may make it easier to get to know your protégé—though you shouldn't take this for granted. But even if you are matched with a protégé with whom you don't have much in common, you can still build a close, trusting relationship—you may just need extra time to get to know each other.

Mentoring an adult from a different cultural, racial or socioeconomic background requires the same kind of awareness that you need to teach and care for children from different backgrounds. You must be aware of how differences between you may stand in the way of understanding and communicating, and you will need to think about each other's learning styles. Differences in backgrounds can also make the relationship with your protégé especially rich. You can both enjoy the opportunity to learn about and support different ways of learning and knowing.

Establishing Expectations and Setting Goals[1]

You can get your relationship with protégés off to a good start by being clear about expectations. At your first meeting, discuss your own roles and responsibilities, and ask the protégé to share hers. (See "Mentors' Expectations for the Mentoring Relationship," on page 66, as well as Activity 1.) Also, discuss when and where you will next meet, and what type of meeting schedule you would ideally like to have. Many find it helpful to write this information down for later reference. Taking the time to talk about these issues at the start can avoid confusion later down the road.

Once you and your protégé have shared expectations, you will be ready to agree to specific goals for your relationship. Goals should focus on two issues:

1) the specific *content area* which will be central to your work with your protégé, or a particular curriculum area such as blocks or group time; and

2) the *structure of the relationship*— when, where and how often you will meet.

Content areas

The content area(s) you work on with the protégé will depend on her experience and prior training, as well as your own skills. Remember that your skills will be changing over time, and you may be able to mentor others in a number of content areas. To provide examples of the possibilities, one mentoring program compiled the following list of activities that mentors and protégés have done together during the past two years.[2]

* rearranging the classroom or home environment;

* observing specific children together, and

---

1 Adapted with permission from Newton et al. (1994), "Establishing Clear Expectations is Critical," 3-5.

2 Adapted with permission from the Minnesota Child Care Apprentice/Mentor Program, Minneapolis, Minn.

"I was looking forward to having a mentee but I didn't realize what I would learn from her. My mentee was one of those people who sees the shining light in the most challenging child. It really helped me to see some of the children differently through her eyes. I have been given at least as much as I have received."

then discussing which developmental issues each child is mastering;

* helping the protégé with homework for an early childhood education class;

* going together to field trip sites in advance to check them out and make arrangements;

* observing the mentor in the classroom or home;

* observing the protégé in the classroom or home;

* setting up an art activities or science area;

* working on children's Individual Education Plans;

* generating ideas to talk about with a special needs coordinator;

* reviewing a resource book or article together;

* planning curriculum activities to match children's developmental needs;

* writing letters for funding or child care advocacy;

* reorganizing a supply closet;

* visiting other child care programs;

* putting together a notebook, with separate sections for each child, for recording observations and anecdotal information;

* collecting and/or purchasing materials;

* writing in journals;

* reading to each other from journals.

One mentor/protégé team in the program worked together on a photo project to help explain to parents how to have developmentally appropriate expectations for their children. During their weekly conferences, they took pictures of children in a variety of activities, including some that frequently annoy parents—such as spilling while pouring juice, putting shoes on the wrong feet, asking "Why?," and jumping off anything that they can climb onto. They then displayed the photos with explanations of how children are developing and learning in these various situations.

The structure of the relationship: Finding time and space to meet

In a child care setting, it can be challenging to find time for adults to meet together. Mentoring relationships, however, require

MENTORS' EXPECTATIONS FOR THE MENTORING RELATIONSHIP

As your mentor:

➤ I will be available to you.

➤ I will help, support and encourage you in managing your work load, and setting up routines.

➤ We will work together to solve problems related to your caregiving career that are important to each of us.

➤ We will treat each other with respect, for example, by keeping appointments, completing assignments, and meeting other agreed-upon expectations.

➤ I will observe your interactions with children and provide you with feedback that will help inform your teaching practice.

➤ Although I do not have "all the answers," I will help you frame the questions that will lead you to your own answers and questions.

➤ I will share with you and demonstrate what I have learned about working with young children.

➤ I will treat everything that occurs in our mentoring relationship with confidentiality.

➤ We will learn from and with each other.

➤ I will not interfere with your relationships with your supervisor or clients.

Source: Adapted with permission from Saphier, J. and R. Gowner (1987), *The Skillful Teacher: Building Your Teaching Skills*. Carlisle, MA: Research for Better Teaching.

regular, uninterrupted opportunities for conversation and planning. Time is critical in new relationships and in learning to understand another person. If you are part of a formal mentoring program, the program coordinator should help arrange opportunities for you and your protégé to meet regularly, working out the details of release time, substitute coverage, schedules and any other logistical matters. If you are having difficulty finding time and a place to meet, be sure to let them know.

During your first meeting, you and your protégé should develop a preliminary plan for conferencing and visiting each other's classrooms or homes. Which times will be most convenient, and how often should you meet? In some cases, the mentoring program will already have guidelines about what is expected. As the relationship progresses, you, your protégé and the program coordinator should check in regularly with each other about how well the time and space arrangements are working, and whether anything needs to be modified.

You should also know that, under the federal Fair Labor Standards Act (FLSA), mentors' and protégés' working time must be fairly compensated. If you are not considered a consultant and do not have exempt status under the FLSA (i.e., you are not an administrator or supervisor), then you, along with your protégé, must be paid time-and-a-half for any hours over 40 worked in a given week.

Supporting Each Other: What Protégés and Mentors Need[3]

While working with you, protégés will need to learn the ropes of teaching and caregiving in their work environment, and what practices do and don't work well with children. They will need to explore whether they like their new role, and whether they want to continue teaching and caring for young children in a group setting.

As a mentor you will play an important role in building protégés' confidence in their abilities, and providing a realistic perspective on their strengths and limitations. In addition, there are a number of things that mentors can do to support protégés:

* Be available to talk with them when upsetting or confusing events and/or interactions happen. Act as a sounding board

---

[3] Adapted with permission from Newton et al. (1994), "How Do You Sponsor New Teachers?," 3-5 to 3-8.

TRAINING AND SUPPORT FOR MENTORS AND PROTÉGÉS

Training and support for mentors and protégés alike is most powerful when:

→ it is practical and related to specific needs;

→ it offers opportunities to discuss concerns;

→ it is followed up by activities which allow practice of new skills and knowledge;

→ it is arranged at times and places that do not conflict with other demands;

→ it occurs frequently enough to sustain interest and engagement;

→ it provides rewards such as credit or increased compensation.

Adapted from Wagner, L, Ward, B., and Dianda, M (1990) "Policy Research in Teacher Education and Staff Development: Dilemmas and Challenges." Paper presented at the Annual Meeting of the American Education Research Association, Boston, as printed in Newton et al. (1994), 2-7.

---

for protégés to vent frustrations without being judged. You may not always agree with your protégé, but you can make sure she has an opportunity to express her point of view, and you can help her resolve or understand events.

* Help protégés in planning their own preparation time, managing stress, and identifying and locating resources.

* Model effective interactions with peers and superiors, participation in program decision making, and sharing ideas, materials and experiences with others.

As a mentor, you also have needs that you will bring to the mentoring relationship. If you are new to teaching adults, you may share many of the insecurities and concerns of new teachers and providers identified in Unit 4.

You may worry about whether you have the necessary skills to help someone else become an effective teacher or provider, and may worry that the protégé will see only your weaknesses instead of recognizing your strengths. You might also question whether or not you will actually like the mentoring role, and how you will benefit from it.

In some mentoring programs, mentors have instructors or field supervisors they can turn to for support. *Mentor support groups* are also a valuable way for mentors to help each other identify and meet their needs for support, recognition and encouragement, and they are an important feature of many mentoring programs. If there is no mentor support group within your program or community, you may wish to join with others to form one.

As you learn skills for assessing adults' needs and strategies for providing feedback, you will begin to decide whether teaching adults is a role you want to continue, and if so, how you can build your strengths as a mentor or trainer. Units 6, 7 and 8 are focused on how to build the skills you need.

The Stages of Mentor/Protégé Relationships

A mentoring relationship, like any formal learning situation, will typically go through various stages. The relationship evolves over time as each person's level of skill and confidence changes, their needs for support shift, and the partners eventually move on, "let go," or change the nature of their relationship.

Tharp and Gallimore (1988) have identified a four-stage teacher training model which can be applied to the stages of mentoring. These stages are not a one-time occurrence, but are repeated throughout one's development as new challenges and tasks present themselves. Thus, the process described below could be repeated in a number of areas during the course of a mentoring relationship, and your protégé could be at different stages for different competencies.

Stage One begins when a person is assisted by someone more capable in performing a task or developing a skill. For example, you might help a new teacher or provider accomplish a defined task, such as reading a story to a group of children. Assistance can come in many forms, including modeling appropriate actions, offering feedback, and prompting reflective questioning. Typically, the mentor/protégé conference (see Unit 6) is the way you will communicate about various strategies, skills, and options for improvement. By the end of this stage, with your help, the protégé might progress from being focused mainly on how to get the children's attention, or finish the story with minimal interruptions, to seeing that she can use stories as a way to spur children's thinking and creativity about a particular topic.

As the protégé's horizons begin to expand, her needs will shift, and she will typically take more responsibility in tailoring to her own needs the type and amount of help she receives from you. During this process, she may experience frustrations—at first, because you might be challenging her to try things beyond her actual level of development, and later, because she has begun to raise her own goals higher, and recognizes how much more there is to learn.

Stage Two begins when the protégé can primarily direct herself in performing an activity or completing a task, while your role or responsibility decreases. At first, as she

stretched toward a higher level of development by assuming new challenges, she may have needed consistent and frequent feedback from you. But by now, she may have a clearer idea of the type of discussion she wants to have with the children about the story—or may even make a plan for acting it out with them, in costume—with relatively little prompting on your part. While she has not completely developed the skills she needs, she is able to work more independently in mastering a task.

By *Stage Three*, performing the task has become more "automatic" for the protégé. She has a well-integrated approach to reading and discussing stories with children, assumes responsibility for such activities, and no longer needs to collaborate with you to carry them out successfully. During this phase, feedback from a mentor might even be disruptive and unwanted.

But like children, adults are not immune to stresses that challenge their abilities or their confidence about even the most well-integrated skills. In *Stage Four*, occasional retraining or other forms of support may be needed for the protégé to "re-fuel" herself if regression or faltering occur. The protégé may be able to help herself by "talking herself through" a problem, but she may need to check in with you for feedback or reassurance.

During this time, the formal nature of your relationship may also begin to alter—either because the mentoring period is coming to an end, the opportunity to meet is decreased, or changes within one or both of you have occurred that make a "separation" process appropriate.

Finally, you and your protégé will work together through a "redefinition" process, during which the relationship either ends or develops into an ongoing, more peer-like form. While "letting go" is not always easy in such a close working relationship, you can both feel gratified that your work together has made a difference in raising your teaching and caregiving practices to a new level of excellence.

Activity 1: Establishing Expectations

Read "Mentors' Expectations for the Mentoring Relationship" on page 66. Do you think these are realistic expectations? How would you change this list? Is there anything you would add or delete?

Activity 2: Identifying Protégés' Needs

Some protégés will be working in a center or family child care home for the first time. Others will be experienced newcomers who have worked previously in a child care setting. Think about how first-time teachers and providers will be the same or different from each other and from experienced newcomers.

➤ What are things that all will need to know?

➤ What special information will "first-timers" need?

Think about different types of information, such as safety procedures, how to find or order supplies, sharing information with parents, etc. For each type, make a list of useful information for protégés. If you can't easily come up with ideas, think back to your first days as a teacher or provider, and what you wish someone had told you. If you do this activity with other mentors, they may think of things you have overlooked.

Activity 3: Taking the Pulse of Your Mentoring Relationship

Taking time to evaluate your relationship is time well spent. The following are activities for reflecting on important aspects of your work with your protégé.

➤ **Mentoring Checklist.** Complete the checklist on the following page at the beginning of, and at several points throughout, your mentoring experience. In addition to checking the box which describes your mentoring behaviors, write down specific examples for each item. ("I show confidence in my protégé. Example: I asked her to take responsibility for group time twice this week.") If you feel comfortable doing so, you may want to discuss your checklist with another mentor, or with your supervisor or mentoring program coordinator.

➤ **Protégé Feedback.** It's also important that you provide some opportunity for your protégé to give you feedback in a written form, in addition to any questions or issues you discuss in person. Sometimes it is too difficult for protégés to tell you how they feel about your relationship. Ask protégés to complete the Protégé Questionnaire (Appendix 7).

➤ Complete the **Mentor Questionnaire** (Appendix 6).

TAKING THE PULSE OF YOUR RELATIONSHIP:
A CHECKLIST FOR MENTORS

❏ **N = never**　　❏ **S = sometimes**　　❏ **F = frequently**　　❏ **A = always**

N S F A

❏ ❏ ❏ ❏　I accept my protégé as a unique individual.

❏ ❏ ❏ ❏　I help my protégé feel she belongs in the program and in the profession.

❏ ❏ ❏ ❏　I show confidence in my protégé.

❏ ❏ ❏ ❏　I let my protégé know I care about her.

❏ ❏ ❏ ❏　I make my protégé feel she has something to contribute.

❏ ❏ ❏ ❏　I sense that my protégé is comfortable bringing problems to me.

❏ ❏ ❏ ❏　I let my protégé express her feelings and ideas.

❏ ❏ ❏ ❏　When I meet with my protégé, I listen more than I speak.

❏ ❏ ❏ ❏　I live up to the agreements we have made.

❏ ❏ ❏ ❏　I keep information about my protégé confidential.

❏ ❏ ❏ ❏　I provide her with resources for developing constructive ideas.

❏ ❏ ❏ ❏　I offer constructive feedback based on observational data.

❏ ❏ ❏ ❏　I respectfully and actively listen to and consider her point of view.

❏ ❏ ❏ ❏　I continually seek to improve my ability to assess others in a just and impartial way.

❏ ❏ ❏ ❏　I refrain from negative comments and making misinformed judgments about others.

❏ ❏ ❏ ❏　I treat my protégé without prejudice.

❏ ❏ ❏ ❏　I continually seek to improve my professional and interpersonal skills.

❏ ❏ ❏ ❏　I model self-reflection.

❏ ❏ ❏ ❏　I nurture my protégé's self-reflection.

❏ ❏ ❏ ❏　I volunteer my special skills.

❏ ❏ ❏ ❏　I am proud of my profession.

❏ ❏ ❏ ❏　I evaluate the attitudes and activities of my protégé with an open mind.

❏ ❏ ❏ ❏　I encourage the personal and professional growth of my protégé.

❏ ❏ ❏ ❏　I am kind and tolerant.

❏ ❏ ❏ ❏　I feel competent to help my protégé in the areas where it is most needed.

❏ ❏ ❏ ❏　I help my protégé identify her strengths and build upon them in new or difficult situations.

❏ ❏ ❏ ❏　I respect my protégé's supervisory line, and her relationships with client families.

Adapted with permission from Newton et al. (1994), "Taking the Pulse on Your Relationship: A Checklist for Mentors," 3-67 to 3-68.

Cassidy, D.J. and Myers, K. (1993). "Mentoring in Inservice Training for Child Care Workers." *Child and Youth Care Forum* 22(5), 387-397.

Newton, A., Bergstrom, K., Brennan, N., Dunne, K., Gilbert, C., Ibarguen, N., Perez-Selles, M. and Thomas, E.(1994). *Mentoring: A Resource and Training Guide for Educators*. Andover, MA: The Regional Laboratory for Educational Improvement.

Tharp, R., and Gallimore, R. (1988). *Rousing Minds to Life: Teaching, Learning and Schooling in Social Context*. New York: Cambridge University Press.

SKILLS FOR EFFECTIVE MENTORING

Mentors are outstanding practitioners who are able to demonstrate excellent skills with young children, families and other adults in the work environment. First and foremost, you are expected to be an excellent role model and to cultivate a supportive, trusting, encouraging relationship with your protégé.

You have been selected to be a mentor not only because of your skills, but because you have a *disposition* for working with children and other adults. A disposition is your inclination towards others or your "frame of mind" about your work. It also means your temperament or patterns of behavior toward people, things or activities.

Mentors and protégés have many different dispositions. Most mentors go above and beyond basic professional practice to include positive attitudes and habits with young children, their families and colleagues. They like their work, and it shows. These characteristics are very important to successful mentoring. They are as important as acquiring other kinds of skills. Mentors can help protégés improve their dispositions in early childhood settings. Mentors who have positive dispositions:

* are delighted with and curious about children's development;

* value children's play;

* expect and embrace continuous change and challenge;

* are willing to take risks and make mistakes;

* make time for regular reflection and self-examination;

* seek collaboration (teamwork) with others and peer support;

* are alert to maintaining professional standards.[1]

When mentors and protégés share a positive approach to their work, relationships can aim to reach their fullest potential. Dispositions relate to all aspects of core knowledge in mentoring, including the skills for effective mentoring contained in this unit:

* communication,

* modeling,

* giving and receiving feedback,

---

[1] Adapted with permission from Carter & Curtis (1994), "Clarifying Core Dispositions," 69-85.

* observation, coaching and conferencing,

* self-assessment,

* resolving conflict, and

* avoiding burnout.

Communication

Each day in a child care program is full of all kinds of communication. Interactions occur constantly between you and children, parents, colleagues and others. Communication does not mean only talking—it means a lot more. Listening, writing, watching, moving and speaking are some of the many ways that humans communicate with each other. We speak in various languages, on the phone, in the media, in letters, on computers, and face-to-face.

Your openness to a range of types of communication will help you to be an effective mentor. Mentors need to know how to listen well and to engage in "active listening." This is a form of communication that makes the person who is speaking to you feel "heard." Active listening involves "playing back" some of the information you hear to the person speaking.

For instance, a protégé says: "I just can't figure out how to lead circle time so that all the children will be involved!" The mentor's response might be, "It sounds like some children are *not* involved in circle. What have you tried to do to engage them?"

In this scenario, the protégé is likely to feel that she was listened to carefully, and that the listener (mentor) wants to help and cares about what happens. The protégé is likely to appreciate this and to feel more motivated to try to solve the problem.

There are five sets of communication skills essential to building satisfying mentor/protégé relationships:[2]

Listening skills ➡ These methods enable a person to really understand what another person is saying. When people feel "listened to," they are often more capable of generating solutions to problems on their own.

> ☛ *Example:* It sounds like you're finding transition times to be the most difficult part of your day. Can you tell me more about what makes them hard?

Assertion skills ➡ These verbal and non-verbal behaviors enable you to get your needs

---

[2] Adapted with permission from Bolton, R. (1979), "Skills for Bridging the Interpersonal Gap," 12.

ACTIVE LISTENING

Requires: attention, with
              congruent body
              language
              acknowledgment
              paraphrasing
              summarizing

**Allows   suggest solutions
others   to be tried
to:**   form their own
                  interpretations
               draw their own
                  inferences

met without manipulation or controlling others. Assertion is not aggression. It is a way to be forthright without bullying. An appropriately assertive person is skilled at using "I" statements to express feelings and needs directly, without blaming or attacking.

☛ *Example:* I know you prefer to meet on Tuesdays at 2:00, but I'm finding it inconvenient. It seems we have to rush our meetings a bit so I can go pick up my son at school. Can we find another time that would work for both of us?

Conflict resolution skills ⇒ See the section of this Unit devoted to this topic on page 83. Relationships can actually be strengthened if these skills are used well.

☛ *Example:* I'm having a hard time giving you feedback about my observations, because you seem kind of defensive. Maybe we have a misunderstanding about the kinds of support and feedback we're each looking for and not looking for. Can we talk about that some more, and try to reach some common ground?

Collaborative problem-solving skills ⇒ These skills incorporate a team approach to solutions which help assure that problems stay solved, and that more people are invested in the solutions.

☛ *Example:* Before we make any decisions, let's come up with a list of all the things we can think of to improve the outdoor play area. Then we can select the options we prefer and make a plan together.

"Each week we talk about classroom experiences, concerns or questions, my protégé's classroom experience, what is working and what is not, specific children, parent interactions, and staff relationships. We try to keep a handle on balance and how to avoid burnout. Respect is the key. I respect my protégé's ability to know herself and to know what she is ready for. I can gently challenge her, but she is the only one who can determine whether the challenge is accepted."

Skill selection ➠ This is the ability to judge which of the communication styles will work best, based on the situation you are in.

☛ *Example:* I know you'd like me to suggest an answer to this problem, but I think that's premature. I'd rather listen more first, and ask you some questions about how you're feeling, because I have a hunch you're already close to deciding what you want to do.

Mentors, ideally, are adept in all five of these skill areas. They are able to put each of them into use freely and offer choices to protégés. Mentors who model positive communication skills to protégés are imparting some essential and lasting lessons.

Modeling

Modeling is a method which mentors use to demonstrate excellent practices to their protégés. Modeling appropriate practices is a profound way to educate someone. When mentors show protégés how to successfully implement curriculum (for example, more culturally sensitive practices), the protégé has learned a new model of instruction with young children. Of course, it is always important to discuss the practices after the modeling has taken place, so that the protégé can adapt them to her own approach.

Occasionally a protégé can ask the mentor to model an appropriate practice in the protégé's home or center. This exchange can be very useful for both mentor and protégé, but needs to be carefully introduced to the children.

Modeling is a strategy that can be very useful in interactions with adults as well. Mentors may choose to offer positive examples for protégés in relating to parents, such as modeling friendly ongoing communication at the beginning and end of the day as parents arrive. Mentors may also guide protégés in staff meeting discussions by offering ways to ask the right questions, or offer helpful suggestions when planning curriculum.

Giving and Receiving Feedback

The art of giving and receiving feedback in a mentor/protégé relationship isn't always easy. Especially at first, protégés may feel inexperienced or sensitive about learning from a veteran about ways to improve their practices. Some mentors are just learning about how to offer help and suggestions for change, and they may fumble. Remembering that it's a "two-way street" will help you to work out supportive methods for communicating without some of the tension that frequently accompanies traditional evaluations by supervisors.

If mentors and protégés use communication skills that are respectful and culturally sensitive, they can accomplish a lot. Mentors should allow time and encourage protégés to speak up about what they need and want from the meeting. A formal structure can assist in this process, but informal ways of giving and receiving feedback should be cultivated, too—for example, phone calls, a short walk at break time, or a breakfast meeting.

Observation, Coaching and Conferencing

Unit 3 presented the process of *reflective conferencing* as a method to use in reflective practice. Observation and coaching are skills that are part of reflective conferencing.

These parts of mentoring have the most to do with the actual teaching of young children in a center or a home.

The word *coach* implies a sense of guiding, or helping to facilitate (move along) the process of learning from an experience. As coaches, mentors provide protégés with opportunities to ask questions, but also model *how to ask questions* that convey how they look at their own teaching. This is known as "modeling inquiry." Mentors do this at the beginning of their relationship with protégés, and throughout the relationship.

The coaching process begins when the mentor and protégé agree about some aspect of their knowledge or practice to work on together. Generally, an observation is set up for the mentor to observe the protégé in her classroom or home. The coaching involves the "art of asking questions" before and after the observation. The two meet prior to the planned observation. This meeting should be at least 30 minutes long and should be free from distractions or interruptions.

The following are sample questions for a *pre-observation conference*.[3] The mentor asks the protégé:

---

[3] Adapted with permission from Newton et al. (1994), "Components of a Pre-Observation Conference," 3-173.

* What is the purpose of this observation?

* What will you be doing with the children?

* What is the curriculum plan?

* What has led up to/will follow this plan?

* What child behaviors do you hope to see/hear?

* What do you want the children to get out of this activity?

* What teaching strategies will you use?

* What do you want me to focus on?

* How shall I document the information?

The mentor records the answers and the two agree on the amount of time the observation will take. The observation should focus on the agreed-upon information supplied by the protégé, not extra information that hasn't been discussed in advance.

The mentor/observer should view the protégé's setting from a discreet location as far away from the "action" as possible, but still be able to hear clearly what is being said. It is the observer's responsibility to do what was agreed upon in the conference and to complete the task within the time frame agreed upon.

The following are sample questions for a *post-observation conference.*[4] The mentor asks the protégé:

* How did you feel about the activity? Why?

* How would you describe what happened with the children?

* How do you feel about what you did?

* How did your behavior/strategies differ from what you planned?

* Do you feel the goals were achieved? Why? Why not? (Mentor provides data here.)

* What have you learned from this?

* What would you do differently next time?

At the end, the mentor and protégé then reflect on the observation and conference to learn what has been most useful and how it all went. You might agree to schedule a follow-up meeting, or set a general time to do another observation in the future.

---

[4] Adapted with permission from Newton et al. (1994), "Components of a Post-Observation Conference," 3-175.

Resolving Conflict[5]

Conflict is an unavoidable part of human change and growth. In the same way, learning to deal with conflict is an unavoidable part of mentoring and teaching. As a teacher or provider, you may find yourself continually faced with conflicts of various kinds among adults and children, and with the need to negotiate. Knowing about effective models of conflict resolution can help you turn difficult situations into opportunities for learning.

A variety of conflicts can emerge within a mentoring situation. As a mentor, you might find yourself confronted by disgruntled colleagues who question the value of the program and the time it takes to be a mentor. Management staff might try to gain your input for the purpose of evaluating a new staff member or provider, even though your mentoring relationship is confidential[6] and non-supervisory in nature. Your protégé might resist your advice and become more difficult to deal with—or on the other hand, might be too dependent, and demand most if not all of your time. Regardless of the situation, there are particular strategies and skills that you can use.

The ability to negotiate is essential to the resolution of conflict. Through their work on the Harvard Negotiation Project, Fisher, Ury and Patton (1991) have developed a model for what they call "principled negotiation" or "getting to yes," as opposed to traditional models which they call "hard" and "soft" negotiation. In "hard" negotiation, opposing sides dig hard into their positions and remain inflexible, each waiting for the other to yield. In "soft" negotiation, participants tend to avoid personal conflict and will often give in—leading to a "resolution" that leaves them feeling resentful and put-upon.

In contrast, "principled negotiation" focuses on principles, rather than on personalities or on winning or losing. "The method of principled negotiation," as Fisher, Ury and Patton describe it, "is to decide issues on their merits rather than through a haggling process focused on what each side says it will

---

[5] Adapted with permission from Newton et al. (1994), "What Skills Do Mentors Need in Resolving Conflict?," 3-33.

[6] Confidentiality pertains to the majority of mentor/protégé interactions. However, as discussed in Unit 2 ("Differences Between Mentoring and Supervision"), when the mentor suspects that the protégé's actions or practice jeopardize the safety and well-being of children, the mentor has an obligation to report allegations to the proper authority.

CONFLICT RESOLUTION:
THE "PRINCIPLED NEGOTIATION" MODEL

PROBLEM		SOLUTION
Positional Bargaining: Which "Game" Should You Play?		Change the "Game" Negotiate on Merits
SOFT	HARD	PRINCIPLED
Participants are friends	Participants are adversaries	Participants are problem solvers
The goal is agreement	The goal is victory	The goal is a wise outcome reached efficiently and amicably
Make concessions to cultivate the relationship	Demand concessions as a condition of the relationship	Separate the people from the problem
Be soft on the people and the problem	Be hard on the people and the problem	Be soft on the people, hard on the problem
Trust others	Distrust others	Proceed independent of trust
Change your position easily	Dig into your position	Focus on interests, not positions
Make offers	Make threats	Explore interests
Disclose your bottom line	Mislead as to your bottom line	Avoid having a bottom line
Accept one-sided losses to reach agreement	Demand one-sided gains as the price of agreement	Invent options for mutual gain
Search for the single answer: the one *they* will accept	Search for the single answer: the one *you* will accept	Develop multiple options to choose from; decide later
Insist on agreement	Insist on your position	Insist on using objective criteria
Try to avoid a contest of will	Try to win a contest of will	Try to reach a result based on standards independent of will
Yield to pressure	Apply pressure	Reason and be open to reason; yield to principle, not pressure

Adapted with permission from Newton et al. (1994), 3-199.

and won't do. It suggests that you look for mutual gains whenever possible, and that where your interests conflict, you should insist that the result be based on some fair standards independent of the will of either side. The method of principled negotiation is hard on the merits, soft on the people. It employs no tricks and no posturing. Principled negotiation shows you how to obtain what you are entitled to and still be decent. It enables you to be fair while protecting you against those who would take advantage of your fairness." (See the accompanying chart, based on these authors' work.)[7]

Being a supportive mentor will take practice in becoming conscious of the messages you send. Knowing how your own behavior might be contributing to the conflict is essential before the conflict can be peacefully resolved. Because of your role as an experienced guide, you will often need to take the lead in modeling behavior that allows principled negotiation to happen. You cannot necessarily change the other person, but you can change your response to the other person's behavior—and in this way, have a better chance of effecting change in that behavior.

---

[7] Fisher et al. (1991).

The following is another example of a simple model for conflict resolution. (This process includes choosing a facilitator and a note-taker.)

* Acknowledge that the problem or conflict exists.

* Define the problem. Allow each party to propose a definition, while the other listens respectfully without interrupting. Seek a definition that both parties can agree on.

* Investigate options for solutions.

* Discuss and examine pros and cons of each option, either generally or point by point.

* Strive for consensus about a strategy for approaching a solution.

* Determine an evaluation period and a process for gauging the success of the action(s) taken.

If you are not successful, revisit the options (step 3), select another strategy, and repeat the steps. Try, try again!

Self-Assessing Practices

Excellent practitioners in early childhood education are aware of their strengths and weaknesses as professionals, and are capable of learning how to make improvements in their practices. Self-assessment tools are a valuable way of developing this kind of awareness of your own work.

Assessing Your Environment

One technique that has proven successful in evaluating early childhood environments in mentoring has been the series of Environmental Rating Scales developed by Harms & Clifford (1980), with different scales for preschool (ECERS), infant/toddler (ITERS), school age (SACERS), and family child care (FDCRS) programs. The Rating Scales allow mentors and protégés to respond to an "objective tool" in assessing classrooms or homes. As an alternative, see the observation forms in Appendix A of *Training Teachers: A Harvest of Theory and Practice* by Carter and Curtis (listed in the References at the end of this Unit). See also Appendix 2 of this *Handbook*, a checklist of health and safety conditions in child care programs.

Assessing Your Own Growth

In Unit 3, we discussed the use of *journals* as an excellent way of charting your own progress and growth as a mentor, and as an avenue for reflection and dialogue between you and your protégé. In addition, or in combination with journals, many mentors also compile *portfolios* of their mentoring experience, which include periodic self-assessments of their progress, needs and goals. Self-assessments can be done on a quarterly basis, or as often as you desire. For a simple self-assessment tool, see the "Self-Evaluation Checklist" in the Activities section of this Unit.

Avoiding Burnout

The "burnout syndrome" is a serious concern in many professions, but especially in one as physically and emotionally challenging as child care. Unrelieved stress, a heavy workload, poor financial rewards, a sense of isolation, the constant turnover of fellow teachers and providers, and insecurity about one's own skills and worth, are all factors that can lead to a loss of control and a lessened capacity to perform one's job.

While burnout takes very individual forms in different people, there are three general characteristics of the syndrome (Jorde-Bloom, 1982):

* emotional and physical exhaustion;

* growing disillusionment with one's job, and perhaps with life in general; and

* self-doubt and blame.

Much of the stress and conflict that teachers and providers feel, of course, is unavoidable—it "comes with the territory." Babies cry; rooms filled with children are noisy; paint and juice have a way of ending up on the floor; people of all ages disagree and argue. It is important to realize that a certain level of stress is positive—it helps human beings to learn, to change, and to face new challenges. The critical task is to avoid becoming overwhelmed or burned out by the things that you *cannot* change, in order to retain the energy to change the things you *can*.

For all the pressures and concerns, not everyone in the child care field succumbs to burnout—quite the opposite. But those who thrive in the profession do so not by accident or luck, but because they have developed certain habits and skills. Many of these have to do with the effective management of time, space, and one's relationships with other people.

To a great extent, mentoring programs have been created in order to help prevent or counteract burnout in the early childhood profession. When mentors and protégés are able to confide in each other and share support, they can relieve worries and self-doubts, and realize that they are not alone.

Mentoring helps experienced teachers and providers to feel recognized and rewarded, and to take on new challenges. Mentoring can also guide new caregivers through the critical first year or two of their work. This is a time when many people who don't have on-the-job support either give up and leave the field, or develop poor work and teaching styles that can lead to burnout down the road.

The Activities section at the end of this chapter contains exercises which can help you and your protégé assess your strengths and challenges, and assess the workplace itself.

Activities

Activity 1: Active Listening

1. Ask your protégé or a fellow mentor to describe a difficulty that she is having. Be sure that she includes:

   - a description of the situation;

   - why she is having trouble with it;

   - any details that help convey the roles of others connected to the problem.

       *

2. Offer her constructive feedback about the situation that demonstrates "active listening" and lets her know that she is being heard. If possible, tape record or videotape this conversation, then play it back together and identify the examples of active listening.

Activity 2: Observation and Conferencing

1. Conduct an observation of your protégé that includes:

   - a pre-observation conference

   - an observation

   - a post-observation conference.

       *

2. Once you have completed the above three-step exercise, examine what worked well. Why did it work well? What could have been done differently?

       *

3. Take notes during this exercise and save them for future reference as you develop more skills. Remember that not every aspect may run smoothly at first; you have the opportunity to try again.

Activity 3: Stress in the Child Care Work Environment

Along with your protégé, select a workplace problem that is common in the child care field, and discuss ways in which you might address it, either individually or together. For example:

➤ The isolation of working in a family child care home.

➤ Finding adequate time for planning, mentoring, training or other professional activities.

➤ The generally low social status and level of respect that is accorded to people who work with young children.

➤ The challenge of balancing work and family responsibilities. (This is a particularly useful discussion for family child care providers, who experience a double use of their home space—for work and for family—each day.)

➤ The high on-the-job exposure to childhood illnesses.

➤ The physical strains of working with children—stooping, bending, lifting, sitting in child-sized rather than adult-sized chairs, etc.

➤ Ways of planning a classroom environment, or of balancing a home/child-oriented environment (in terms of furniture arrangement, lighting, ventilation, storage of toys, materials and equipment, etc.) that promote relaxation and comfort, and relieve stress.

Activity 4: Self-Evaluation (for mentors and protégés)

1. Complete the checklist on pages 91-93 and share the results with your mentor/ protégé.

*

2. Keep a copy on file and redo it quarterly, midway through your mentor/protégé relationship, or on some other regular basis. Ask yourself:

➤ How have you changed? Why?

➤ In what areas do you need to grow?

➤ How will you bring about new growth in yourself and with your mentor/protégé?

*

3. Save notes and documents related to this exercise to track your improvements.

SELF EVALUATION CHECKLIST

I am like this:	This is something I can learn:	When people say, "This is an effective teacher/provider," they mean that she:
		PERSONAL QUALITIES AND PRESENCE
☑	❏	Is relaxed and comfortable, yet alert
☑	❏	Maintains good eye contact, often getting down to a child's eye level
☑	❏	Speaks with a voice that is gentle, quiet, calm and firm; sending messages that are direct and clear
☑	❏	Has a special voice for talking to children
☑	❏	Has a clean, healthy, professional appearance and wears clothes appropriate to the day's work
☑	❏	Listens carefully and respectfully
☑	❏	Has a high tolerance for noise and movement and doesn't expect order every moment
☑	❏	Touches children often with movements that soothe, guide, redirect, reassure, reinforce
		CAREGIVING STYLE AND STRATEGIES
☑	❏	Enjoys children and expresses genuine interest in them
☑	❏	Is willing to learn from children and follow their lead
☑	❏	Is able to focus on individual children while being aware of what is happening throughout the classroom/home
☑	❏	Relates to each child's personality and developmental level
☑	❏	Uses positive statements
☑	❏	Is empathetic—able to show children she can understand the feelings behind their words or behavior
☑	❏	Creates opportunities for one-to-one activities with children
☑	❏	Is aware of differing moods of children, and adjusts standards for them when they are fatigued, irritated, overstimulated, or stressed

I am like this:	This is something I can learn:	When people say, "This is an effective teacher/provider," they mean that she:
☑	☐	Remains in control in difficult situations
☑	☐	Enjoys humorous incidents with children; is able to laugh with them
☑	☐	Has a plan and a set of goals for each day
☑	☐	Sets consistent, realistic limits
☑	☐	Provides guidance in the development of good habits for eating, resting, toileting, learning, exercise
☐	☑	Responsive to children's rhythms and tempos
☑	☐	Honors cultural differences

DESIGN OF LEARNING ENVIRONMENT

☑	☐	Creates an environment where children are comfortable enough to verbalize their feelings
☑	☐	Creates an atmosphere that is comfortable, home-like, safe
☑	☐	Provides an organized, structured schedule to reassure children
☑	☐	Fosters inquisitiveness about physical world
☑	☐	Facilitates social interactions among children
☑	☐	Questions and explores with children so that all learn through discovery
☑	☐	Maintains an organized, clean classroom/home
☑	☐	Considers the outdoors part of the learning environment

RELATIONSHIPS TO OTHER TEACHERS/PROVIDERS

☑	☐	Accepts criticism and is responsive to changes
☑	☐	Gets along well with others
☑	☐	Asks for help when needed
☑	☐	Is quick to express approval and support for co-workers
☑	☐	Can listen to suggestions and ideas, but is not just a "yes" person

I am like this:	This is something I can learn:	When people say, "This is an effective teacher/provider," they mean that she:
☑	❑	Is aware of others' needs in classroom and is prepared to "take over" when necessary
❑	☑	Is slow to make judgments and sensitive in sharing feedback
☑	❑	Leads, shares leadership, and/or steps aside when necessary
☑	❑	Is a team player; involves co-workers in planning

RELATIONSHIP TO PARENTS

❑	☑	Communicates with parents at drop-off and pick-up times, and is available as needed throughout the day
☑	❑	Schedules parent conferences when needed
☑	❑	Does not discuss children's behavior in their presence
☑	❑	Respects families' right to privacy by keeping discussions confidential
☑	❑	Assists parents with goals for their children
☑	❑	Sees role as part of a support system to parents, helping to strengthen families
❑	☑	Helps parents recognize their strengths
❑	❑	Asks parents for their insights about their children

PROFESSIONAL RESPONSIBILITIES

☑	❑	Attends regular staff meetings and workshops
☑	❑	Makes a conscientious effort to expand knowledge of good early childhood care
☑	❑	Is willing to try new things, and to risk making mistakes
☑	❑	Manages time well
☑	❑	Demonstrates pride in being a child care practitioner
☑	❑	Takes advantage of learning opportunities provided

Adapted from a form developed by Exchange Press (Redwood, WA) as a service to its readers.

Bolton, R. (1979). *People Skills*. Englewood Cliffs, NJ: Prentice-Hall, Inc.

Carter, M. and Curtis, D. (1994). *Training Teachers: A Harvest of Theory and Practice*. St. Paul, MN: Redleaf Press.

Fisher, R., Ury, W. and Patton, B. (second edition, 1991). *Getting to Yes*. Boston: Houghton-Mifflin.

Harms, T. and Clifford, R.M. (1980). *Early Childhood Environment Rating Scale*. New York: Teachers College Press.

Jorde-Bloom, P. (1982; reprinted 1989). *Avoiding Burnout: Strategies for Managing Time, Space and People in Early Childhood Education*. Lake Forest, Ill.: New Horizons.

Newton, A., Bergstrom, K., Brennan, N., Dunne, K., Gilbert, C., Ibarguen, N., Perez-Selles, M. & Thomas, E. (1994). *Mentoring: A Resource and Training Guide for Educators*. Andover, MA: The Regional Laboratory for Educational Improvement of the Northeast and Islands.

Shulman, J.H., and Colbert, J.A. (1978). *The Mentor Teacher Casebook*. ERIC Clearinghouse on Educational Management (University of Oregon) and Far West Laboratory for Educational Research and Development.

MENTORS AS LEADERS AND ADVOCATES

Since mentors are called upon to act as leaders and role models for other teachers and providers, building your leadership and advocacy skills is an important part of your training as a mentor. As you build your understanding of adult development and your abilities to communicate with and support protégés, you also build your capacity for leadership. Because you have managed to advance your skills and to achieve a new level of professional status, you signal a sense of possibility and hope to your co-workers about child care as a worthy career option. Your voice, and that of other mentors, can carry a great deal of influence with fellow teachers and providers.

As a core group of skilled and dedicated practitioners, you and other mentors are emerging as effective advocates for the early childhood profession. In a number of communities, mentors have stepped to the forefront of efforts to promote better resources and services for children, and to improve working conditions, training and compensation for their fellow teachers and providers.

When you think about leaders, perhaps the most common dictionary definitions come to mind: a person with commanding authority or influence, someone who goes ahead of others, someone who is in charge or in control. As an alternative, we suggest that a leader is a guide, someone who can help accompany others and show the way. Leaders are also advocates who support and speak for a cause. Even though you may not think of yourself as a "leader," surely anyone who cares skillfully for children has such qualities.

As an effective teacher or provider, you are able to guide the interactions and movements of many people (adults included) through the course of a complex day. Not everyone, for example, could facilitate the transition of a group of children from high-energy outdoor play to a more low-key circle time, lunch period and nap. Not everyone commands the many adult communication skills required of you as you interact with co-workers, parents, volunteers, trainees and other professionals.

In this Unit and in Unit 8, we identify

many of the skills you can use as you embark upon this new professional path. You will be working not only in the children's environment but also helping other adults plan and put into effect a quality program for children. And you can also take part in identifying broader changes to improve environments for children and their caregivers.

Mentors Working for Quality Child Care

Many child care teachers and providers like you face daunting conditions on the job which make it difficult to offer quality care for children and families. Among the most common obstacles are:

* a scarcity of equipment and materials;

* unmanageable adult-child ratios;

* co-workers with little or no training;

* few resources for professional development;

* high staff turnover, which is demoralizing and demanding for those who remain;

* a lack of familiarity with the cultures and/ or home languages of children and families;

* increasing numbers of children and families living in poverty or facing other stresses in family life, such as violence or abuse;

* the practical hardships that accompany working for poverty-level wages and inadequate or non-existent benefits—e.g., no money for a decent car or other transportation, or the need to work when sick because of no health coverage or sick leave; and

* the assault on one's self-esteem that comes from a lack of respect for the skills demanded by the job.

If you have faced (or are facing) any of these problems, you know they make it difficult to do what you think is developmentally appropriate with children. And you know how personally these conditions can affect you. Largely, they stem from our nation's unwillingness to guarantee quality early childhood education opportunities for all children and families, and from the insufficient funding that is typical of many programs.

As a mentor, you may be wondering what you can do to secure better resources for early care and education. You may not know what role you can play. But if our profession's goal

"I was so frustrated as a preschool teacher. I felt that nobody cared about my work, and I was planning to go back to school so I could go into a "real" profession. Then I got involved in the Mentor Teacher Program. It was so great to be with others who saw themselves as professionals; it helped me to see myself that way and to realize that child care is "for real." I want to be a better advocate so that everyone will get a chance to experience the Mentor Program. We need more of us! We need teachers and providers who can advocate for ourselves."

is to ensure the well-being of young children, it is "unprofessional" to allow poor conditions for children to go unchallenged. This means that beyond our direct work with children, we must involve ourselves in efforts to improve the services that are available to them. Along with becoming excellent caregivers, we need to learn about becoming agents of change. We need to learn skills which can help us to reshape the conditions for effective teaching and caregiving.

This may sound like an overwhelming challenge, and one for which you don't feel prepared. But mentors like yourself are among the most effective child care advocates. By demonstrating your skill to your colleagues, and by promoting the importance of your work throughout the community, you build support for improving the quality of services for children and families. In particular, you can be one of the best spokespersons for early childhood careers and the value of mentoring.

To assist you in your role as a leader and advocate, this Unit focuses on helping you to build your understanding of the following issues:

* the current child care delivery system and its consequences;

* how to improve child care work environments;

* why and how practitioners have joined together to address the problems facing their profession.

The Child Care Delivery System and its Consequences

Young children thrive when they are cared for in high-quality early care and education programs. Regardless of their gender, ethnicity or family socioeconomic background, children display more advanced language, pre-math and social skills when they are cared for in higher-quality centers and homes (Cost, Quality and Child Outcomes Team, 1995; Kontos et al., 1995; Whitebook et al., 1990). Children in lower-quality programs, however, tend to wander without purpose, neither involved with people nor with activities.

Despite the clear link between child care quality and children's later well-being, the majority of children in the United States attend early care and education programs that are barely adequate (Cost, Quality and Child Outcomes Team, 1995; Kontos et al., 1995; Whitebook et al., 1993). The quality of care children receive is primarily related to staffing issues. Children's needs cannot be met in centers and homes where there are untrained staff, high staff turnover fueled by low wages, and too many children for each adult. Quality child care requires an environment that values adults as well as children.

For more information in this area, see also Appendices 3 to 5, "Selected Readings About Early Care and Education in the United States," "The National Child Care Staffing Study: Highlights of Major Findings," and "Child Care Work Force Facts."

Improving Your Work Environment

As a mentor, you will be devoting much of your time to helping individual teachers or providers become better educated and trained in early childhood theory and practice. But you will also want to assist them in thinking about how the work environment is organized and structured, and how it influences their ability to provide high-qual-ity services. Regulations governing child care programs typically focus only on the environment as a place for children, with little input about adult needs.

There are two primary ways that you can work with others to assess and upgrade your work environment. The first involves playing an active role in a process such as National Association for the Education of Young Children (NAEYC) or Family Child Care Accreditation. These assessments provide a framework for you, your protégés and other team members to analyze important aspects of your program's structure. The second involves learning about and discussing other issues that affect teachers and providers and that are not directly addressed in the current accreditation systems. For example:

* Are there any on-the-job hazards in your child care setting? How can your environment be changed to reduce adult injuries and stress? (See Appendix 4, "Checklist for Health and Safety Conditions," as well as Activity 3, "Stress in the Child Care Work Environment," in Unit 6 of this *Handbook*, page 89.)

* What are employees' rights on the job? Can providers easily secure qualified substitutes to cover for them when needed?

"I feel valued when I can help someone, and that's why I wanted to be a mentor. Still, I feared I wouldn't be able to go through with the program; I would be too afraid to speak publicly. But the program has encouraged me to find the strength inside of me. It gave me a voice. We need change, and it can't happen unless we are heard."

✳ Are there adequate opportunities and procedures for airing grievances? Are effective communication systems in place between staff and with parents?

As a mentor, you are in a unique position to lead these discussions because you share the same work environment. You can also bring perspectives from other programs in the community to your own program—either by visiting them or by inviting teachers or providers to visit your setting. This exchange can help all members of your team identify strengths in your program as well as make improvements.

Joining with Others Beyond the Workplace to Make Change

If you are like many child care teachers and providers, you may feel fairly isolated on the job. The demands of your work schedule, coupled with family responsibilities, leave little time for visiting other programs or meeting with teachers or providers in other settings. Yet when you do have the opportunity to share your stories with other caregivers, you can find not only that you have a great deal in common, but that your combined voices can be powerful and lead to improvements.

For the past twenty years, a small but growing and dedicated group of teachers and providers has led efforts to address the staffing crisis, calling for training linked to compensation, and greater respect for child care work. Early childhood mentoring programs in several states are the direct result of their efforts. For example, the California Early Childhood Mentor Program, currently the largest in the country, was started by child care teachers who were concerned about the high turnover among skilled caregivers in the field, and the lack of supervised field work options for new teachers and providers.

Advocacy efforts among child care staff and providers have also paved the way for a comprehensive Caregiver Personnel Pay Plan in U.S. Army Child Development Services, policies to upgrade the compensation and training of Head Start teachers, and better resources for teachers and providers in programs funded by various states. This acknowledgment of staff needs resulted from various efforts of teachers and providers, including: research to document the relationship between child care quality and low wages, public education about the nature of child care work, and advocacy for supportive public policies.

There are numerous groups continuing these efforts to improve child care jobs, and they welcome other teachers and providers as members. For although some important gains have been made in recent years, child care work is still the lowest paid of any occupation in the country, and the poor quality of many services has negative consequences for children. If you are interested in getting involved, call or write to any or all of the groups described below. You can also join with other mentors or co-workers to brainstorm ideas about how you can work to improve the image and resources for early care and education jobs and services. Consider:

* public speaking about the significance of child care work in your community;

* promoting mentoring relationships and recruiting mentors;

* starting a support network for mentors and/or protégés;

* building alliances with other child care programs in your community or state;

* becoming actively involved in a local or national early childhood or family child care association;

* writing a letter to the editor of a local newspaper;

* writing to, calling or visiting elected officials and other child care policy makers about issues of child care legislation and funding; and

* any of your own ideas!

☞ The **Center for the Child Care Workforce** (CCW) is a research and advocacy group committed to improving child care by upgrading compensation, working conditions and training opportunities for child care teachers and providers. Along with its biannual newsletter, *Rights, Raises, Respect: News and Issues for the Child Care Work Force,* and other publications, CCW coordinates two projects which may be of particular interest to mentors:

✳ The *Early Childhood Mentoring Alliance* is dedicated to: 1) providing a forum for information exchange among all those who are involved in creating, strengthening and expanding early childhood mentoring programs, 2) serving as an organized voice to advocate for mentoring programs at the local, state and national levels, 3) supporting mentors and program developers through resources and training, and 4) building mentors' skills as leaders and advocates in the field.

✳ The *Worthy Wage Campaign* is a nationwide grassroots effort to empower and mobilize teachers and providers to reverse the child care staffing crisis. It is dedicated to: 1) creating a unified voice for the concerns of the early care and education work force at the local, state and national levels, 2) fostering respect for those who provide early care and education by advocating for better wages, training and working conditions, and 3) promoting accessible and affordable high-quality child care options that meet the diverse needs of families. Launched in 1991, the Worthy Wage Campaign consists of over 200 member groups in 40 states, plus the District of Columbia and Canada.

☞ The **National Association for Family Child Care** (NAFCC) is a membership organization for family child care providers. NAFCC offers insurance for its members and operates a national accreditation project. It also provides members with a newsletter and other educational materials. For more information contact NAFCC, 206 Sixth Avenue, Midland Bldg., Suite 900, Des Moines, IA 50309. (515) 282-8192.

☞ The **National School Age Care Alliance** (NSACA) is a membership organization composed of state coalitions of school-age child care staff, as well as individual staff who are new to the field and seek affiliation with a professional organization. Basic membership benefits include a newsletter, a discount to the annual national school-age child care conference, and access to current information about school-age care. For more information contact NSACA, P.O. Box 676, Washington, DC 20044-0676. (202) 737-NSAC (6722).

☞ The **National Association for the Education of Young Children** (NAEYC) offers professional development opportunities to early childhood educators designed to improve the quality of services to children from birth through age 8. NAEYC's current network of 90,000 members in 450 Affiliate Groups was founded in 1926. NAEYC administers a national, voluntary accreditation system for early childhood centers and schools. Its Professional Development Institute and its Quality, Compensation and Affordability groups focus on improving career options in the field and the quality of services. It publishes *Young Children*, a bimonthly magazine focused on classroom practice, teacher training and advocacy. For more information, contact NAEYC, 1509 16th Ave. NW, Washington, DC 20036-1426, (800) 424-2460.

☛ The **National Latino Children's Agenda** is implemented by leaders from many organizations that are working together to ensure the health and complete development of Latino children. The group works to report on the crisis of Latino children, and to build support for policies that lead to high-quality programs that are respectful of Latino cultural values and language. For more information, contact Corporate Fund for Children, 1611 West Sixth Street, Austin, TX 78703. (512) 472-9971.

☛ The **National Black Child Development Institute** (NBCDI) is a national nonprofit organization dedicated to improving the quality of life for African American children and youth on the national and local levels. Founded in 1970, NBCDI provides direct services to African American children and youth, monitors public policy issues, and educates the public through reports, newsletters and conferences. For more information, contact NBCDI, 1023 15th Street, N.W., Suite 600, Washington, DC 20005. (202) 387-1281.

☛ The **Center for Career Development in Early Care and Education**, founded in 1991 at Wheelock College, strives to improve the quality of care and education for young children by creating viable career development systems for practitioners. The activities of the Center are designed to help states and localities bring about systematic change to replace the fragmented systems of training that now exist. The Center also offers seminars in child care administration. For more information, contact the Center for Career Development in Early Care and Education, Wheelock College, 200 The Riverway, Boston, MA 02215. (617) 734-5200.

Activity 1: The Child Care System and Its Consequences

1. With other mentors, protégés and/or members of your team, discuss the following questions:

   → Why are child care wages lower than in other professions?

   → What are the effects of these lower wages—on me, on the child care profession, on children, on families, on society?

   → What are the obstacles, both structural and personal, to improving child care jobs?

   → How can we overcome these obstacles?

   → What do I need, as an individual, to be able to take action to improve child care jobs?

   *

2. With your co-workers, sketch out a vision of quality child care—both for children and for the adults who care for them.

   → What would really good child care look like?

   → What would good working conditions be?

   → How would it be different from what you now have?

   *

3. Discuss how taking action to improve child care outside the work place connects with teaching and caregiving. Does activism support or take away from your work with children?

Activity 2: Polling

1. Complete an informal survey of five to ten friends, asking them:

   -→ what they think a child care worker does,

   -→ how much money child care workers earn,

   -→ how much child care workers *should* earn,

   -→ how much training child care workers usually have, and

   -→ how much training child care workers need to do their jobs well.

   ✳

2. Discuss your findings with other mentors and protégés, to analyze the views behind different answers people gave.

   ✳

3. Brainstorm ways to provide alternative viewpoints to people with whom you disagree.

Activity 3: Speaking Out for Quality

Child Care Jobs and Programs

We all need opportunities to voice our own opinions, listen to opposing viewpoints, challenge stereotypes and network with others. Start with the activities below that feel most comfortable, and eventually expand your outreach.

✳

1. Write a letter to the editor of the local newspaper, or an article for a child care newsletter, about the mentoring program and the impact it has made in your community. Share personal experiences and a few well-chosen facts.

✳

2. Hold an informational meeting for the community about the benefits gained from the mentoring program. Emphasize the personal stories; these are what move people the most.

✳

3. Develop other ideas for recruiting more teachers and providers into the mentoring program, and/or building community recognition and support for the importance of child care work.

✳

4. Contact the Worthy Wage Campaign for more information on working with the media and public awareness activities.

Bellm, D. (1994). *Breaking the Link: A National Forum on Child Care Compensation.* Washington, DC: Center for the Child Care Workforce.

Bellm, D. and Whitebook, M. (in press). *Leadership Empowerment Action Project (LEAP): A Training Guide for the Early Childhood Community.* Washington, DC: Center for the Child Care Workforce.

Carter, M. and Curtis, D. (1994). *Training Teachers: A Harvest of Theory and Practice.* St. Paul, MN: Redleaf Press.

Cost, Quality, and Child Outcomes Team (1995). *Cost, Quality and Child Outcomes in Child Care Centers: Executive Summary,* January 1995. Denver: Economics Department, University of Colorado at Denver.

Kontos, S., Howes, C., Shinn, M., and Galinsky, E. (1995). *Quality in Family Child Care and Relative Care.* New York: Teachers College Press.

Morgan, G., Azer, S., Costley, J., Genser, A., Goodman I., Lombardi, J., and McGimsey, B. (1993). *Making a Career of It: The State of the States Report on Career Development in Early Care and Education.* Boston: Wheelock College Center for Career Development in Early Care and Education.

National Black Child Development Institute. (1993). *Pathways to African American Leadership Positions in Early Childhood Education: Constraints and Opportunities.* Washington, DC: NBCDI.

Newton, A., Bergstrom, K., Brennan, N., Dunne, K., Gilbert, C., Ibarguen, N., Perez-Selles, M., and Thomas, E. (1994). *Mentoring: A Resource and Training Guide for Educators.* Andover, MA: The Regional Laboratory for Educational Improvement.

Rodd, J. (1995). *Leadership and Early Childhood: A Pathway to Professionalism.* New York: Teachers College Press.

Whitebook, M. (1994). "At the Core: Advocacy to Challenge the Status Quo," in *The Early Childhood Career Lattice: Perspectives on Professional Development,* Johnson, J., and McCracken, J., eds. Washington, DC: National Association for the Education of Young Children.

Whitebook, M. (1997). "Who's Missing at the Table?: Leadership Opportunities and Barriers for Teachers and Providers," in *Rethinking Leadership in Early Care and Education,* Kagan, S.L. and Bowman, B., eds. Washington, DC: National Association for the Education of Young Children.

Whitebook, M., Hnatiuk, P., and Bellm, D. (1994). *Mentoring in Early Care and Education: Refining an Emerging Career Path.* Washington, DC: Center for the Child Care Workforce.

Whitebook, M., Howes, C., and Phillips, D. (1990). *Who Cares? Child Care Teachers and the Quality of Care in America: The National Child Care Staffing Study, Final Report.* Washington, DC: Center for the Child Care Workforce.

Whitebook, M., Phillips, D. and Howes, C. (1993). *The National Child Care Staffing Study Revisited: Four Years in the Life of Center-based Child Care.* Washington, DC: Center for the Child Care Workforce.

Whitebook, M., Bellm, D., Nattinger, P, and Pemberton, C. (1990). *Working for Quality Child Care: An Early Childhood Education Text.* Washington, DC: Center for the Child Care Workforce.

PLANNING A LEARNING SESSION FOR ADULTS

Amidst the flurry of activity in a well-run child care center classroom or family child care home, there is a sense of order—even on a difficult day. Children know what to expect, and are quick to notice any change in routine. They feel confident that everyone will get a turn, whether it's to talk during circle time or to try the new paints. Enter a poor-quality program and the reverse is true: children are scattered, unfocused, and anxious that they will be overlooked.

While a high-quality home or classroom environment looks effortless, we all know how much planning it takes to create a smooth-running program for children. Similarly, a well-run meeting or workshop for adults doesn't just happen because a group of adults come together. Thoughtful preparation and clarity of purpose are necessary to create an experience for adults in which all participants feel free to express themselves, explore new ideas and practice new skills.

As you grow professionally as a mentor, you may find yourself called upon to consider working not only one-to-one with protégés, but with *groups* of adults—whether as a workshop leader, meeting facilitator or trainer. This Unit is devoted to the skills that are involved in such group work.

The Adult Learning Environment

As Margie Carter and Deb Curtis suggest in their book, *Training Teachers: A Harvest of Theory and Practice,* "We teach teachers in the ways consistent with how we want them to teach the children in their care....If we want teachers to provide opportunities for children to explore and make their own discoveries, these possibilities must be provided for them as adults."

In designing a learning environment for adults, it's important to keep in mind the principles of adult development we discussed in Unit 3—namely, that adults:

* respond to training that is relevant to their lives;

* learn best by building on what they already know;

* seek respect and acknowledgment for their life experiences;

* process information in different ways depending on their learning styles and backgrounds;

* learn best when they are actively engaged; like children, they "learn by doing."

Curtis and Carter design training and meetings based on four assumptions reflecting adult development. These can serve as your guide for your own work with protégés:

* Participants bring their own knowledge, experiences and learning styles to any training session.

* Existing knowledge and experiences are the sources of new learning. With adults, the concrete materials and experiences we focus on are their daily lives, ideas, understandings and values.

* From the outset, training should help caregivers and providers find their own voice and foster reflection and problem-solving.

* Each training requires a variety of activities to address the different learning styles and intelligence of the participants.

Carter and Curtis's approach requires continual analysis, reflection and adjustment on the part of the facilitator—the very skills you, as a mentor, are helping protégés to build in their work with children. They recommend "Five Examinations" to consider in planning or evaluating your work with adult learners:

1. Examine your own views: What experiences and conditioning do you bring to this teaching situation? Are you aware of the kinds of environment in which you feel most comfortable? Who is comfortable in the environment you have created?

2. Examine the environment: How is it influencing the learning that occurs?

3. Examine child development: How does the session relate to providing optimal experiences for children?

4. Examine issues of diversity: What assumptions, biases or limiting factors are at work?

5. Examining your roles and strategies: How can you be more responsive and skillful?

Steps in Planning a Meeting or Training Session

The ability to create a learning atmosphere

in which people can grow and discover themselves involves thoughtful planning. Although in the next section we will focus on planning a single session, it is important to remember that education is a continuing process, not a one-time event. The process outlined below can guide the planning of all workshops and meetings with protégés, and with other teachers and providers.

Steps for Planning a Meeting or Training Session

Step 1: Assess needs

Step 2: Develop objectives

Step 3: Develop an agenda and select methods

Step 4: Make necessary arrangements

Step 5: Implement the session

Step 6: Evaluate

Step 7: Follow up

☛ **Step 1. Assess needs**

At first, your trainer or mentoring program coordinator may suggest topics that protégés might seek or need information about. They might also help you develop strategies for

---

Sample One Hour Workshop or Meeting Format

(from Carter and Curtis)

➥ Welcome, introductions, overview of agenda
(5-10 minutes)

➥ Opening activity to reflect on topic
(10 minutes)

➥ Presentation of core ideas
(10-15 minutes)

➥ Practice applying ideas
(15-20 minutes)

➥ Next steps and follow-up
(5 minutes)

➥ Summary and evaluation
(5 minutes)

---

choosing specific topics and appropriate levels of information for a protégé training session. You can learn a great deal about protégés' needs through observations or surveys, and by reviewing the Environmental

"The Mentor Program came at a critical point. I was ready to leave the field. I felt like the Program said to me, "You are a teacher, a professional and an advocate," and it helped me recognize that I have those skills. I have met so many people, and so many opportunities have opened up."

Rating Scales or other rating materials. You might also talk with protégés or other participants directly about what they want to know and their current level of knowledge.

☞ **Step 2. Develop objectives**

Education or training objectives can be identified using information you gather from the needs assessments. At the start, your trainer or mentoring program coordinator might help you make decisions about protégés' skill levels and needs. As you become more experienced as an adult educator, you will be able to develop objectives more independently. As experienced trainers know, however, reviewing your objectives and training plans with another colleague almost always results in a more effective session.

It is a common mistake among trainers to assume that the objective of a workshop is simply to present *information* to participants. You will also want sessions to focus on specific *skills and behaviors* that participants need to do their jobs and the *attitudes* that influence their learning. Carter and Curtis suggest selecting one or two big ideas that you want to get across to participants in any session, thinking about how these will relate to

teacher/provider practices with children. Effective objectives reflect shared goals of the trainer/leader and the other participants; time should be set aside in the session to mutually agree to them. Some objectives are easier to achieve than others, and no single strategy or method will work for every type of objective.

☞ **Step 3. Develop an agenda and select methods**

Based on the objectives you have selected, you can now develop the training plan or outline. This step consists of two parts. One is to determine which topics will be covered, and the order of and time allotments for each topic (see box with sample format on page 111). The other is to select the appropriate teaching method or strategy that you will use in the session and to identify any equipment or materials you need.

In selecting teaching methods, it's also important to consider the content area and the profile of participants. Depending on the reading level, language skills, learning styles and experience of your protégés or others, some methods may be more or less helpful. Time limitations are also important to consider. You can usually achieve less in a given amount of training time than you might expect. It is always helpful to provide a good mix of methods. Some, such as lectures or informational films, primarily fulfill information or attitude objectives. Other more comprehensive methods, such as case studies or role plays, may trigger the exploration of attitudes, and encourage more active learning.

If you feel anxious about working with adults in a group setting, it may be that you are carrying an image of a lecturer who speaks to an audience for long periods of time. Lecturing is only one approach, and often one that is relatively unsuccessful. Choosing teaching methods also involves your own skill and comfort level. You may prefer making a short presentation as part of a panel, or stimulating the group to explore a topic instead of a lecture. In most instances, more than one teaching method can, and should, be used to achieve a given objective.

Once you have decided upon methods, you can finalize your outline. The outline is essentially a lesson plan for adults, calling upon many skills you already use in your work with children. The outline should include the purpose of the session, the materials required, the activities, and any assignment that will be given to participants. Your trainer or mentoring program coordinator, or other mentors, can review your outline, and give you feedback about the methods you have chosen, and whether the activities can be completed in the given time frame. As with any lesson plan, an outline is only a guide. If the planned activities aren't working, you will need to shift gears, as you do with children on days when your plans don't seem to mesh with their moods or needs.

☞ **Step Four. Make necessary arrangements**

Wonderful, spontaneous sessions are the exception, not the rule. Smoothly operating learning environments, whether for adults or children, reflect thoughtful prior planning. To avoid problems during training sessions or meetings, consider each of the following issues:

* A date and time for the session is approved by the appropriate person(s).

* A space where participants can easily see and hear each other is approved for use during the training.

* Permission is granted and time allowed for the appropriate arrangement of the space for the training, e.g. adult size chairs are

available, they can be moved into a circle for small group discussions, you know how to adjust the thermostat if necessary, etc.

* Participants are notified of the date, starting and ending time, and location of the training, and substitutes for their classrooms or homes are available if necessary.

* Special materials or equipment (audio-visuals, charts, tape, markers, tape recorders, adequate copies of handouts, coffee pot, food and beverages etc.) are requested or gathered and are known to be in working order.

* Appropriate materials are given to participants in advance.

* A sign-in sheet is provided to document participants' attendance at the session.

☛ Step Five. Implement the session

Conducting an effective session becomes much easier when potential problems have been identified and addressed in advance. As with learning any new skill, practice is the key. It may help you to review the training outline several times before the actual session, and when possible, to try out different activities with other mentors or co-workers. Here are some tips:

* Explain the exercises clearly.

* Draw upon participants' experiences.

* Use humor and stories.

* Be an active listener.

* Encourage, but do not pressure, all participants to become actively involved.

* Use language participants can understand.

* Review what has been said or done.

* Stay flexible.

☛ Step 6. Evaluate

Even if it is limited, there should be an opportunity for evaluation at every session. Structure it so that everyone who wants to can share their reactions. Evaluation serves important purposes for the learner and the educator. It allows the learner to judge his or her progress toward new knowledge, skills, attitudes or actions. It allows the educator to judge the effectiveness of the training and to decide what has been accomplished. Evaluations identify whether the learning objectives have been reached, and which different activities helped in the process.

There are several methods for evaluating sessions. Some people prefer to share or receive comments in writing; others prefer discussion. Your trainer or mentoring program coordinator may be able to help you identify which type of evaluation will provide you with the most useful feedback.

In addition to an evaluation, every session should include a time to make future plans. Before people begin to leave, be sure that you have agreed upon:

* the next meeting time and location;

* any planning responsibilities;

* any tasks that participants have agreed to complete;

* any follow-up activities (see below).

☛ *Step 7. Follow up*

The most effective learning is reinforced over time. With respect to your protégés, this may involve checking in about an assignment given during the session, or arranging to observe in each other's homes or classrooms. You might want to set up another meeting or session on the same or a related topic. By returning to the topic, you provide another chance for participants to clarify their understanding.

Additional Skills for Effective Training

You will rely on a number of other important skills in preparing for group sessions. You need to know how to find information about topics you will be covering. Sessions will be enriched by sharing theory, research and practical examples contained in the early childhood and child development literature. Many of us have outdated library research skills, because we have not yet learned to use computers and the many resources available "on line." Ask your trainer or mentoring program coordinator how to gain access to resources available in the community (e.g. the public library, the local resource and referral agency, the Internet, etc.). Also refer to the list of child care organizations in Unit 7, page 101.

In addition, you will need clear oral and written communication skills in your role as a mentor. You may have different strengths in writing and speaking skills. Your trainer or mentoring program coordinator may be able to help you assess your skills and develop an appropriate training plan.

Activity 1: Identifying Group Sessions That Work

By the time we are adults, we have all had many experience with other adults, whether in meetings, classes, or at church or synagogue. Most of us know what we do and don't like in these settings, and that information can serve as "research data" about effective training and group methods.

On your own, with other mentors or with your protégé, think about group sessions (meetings, training workshops, etc.) that you have enjoyed and felt contributed to your professional growth. Make a list of characteristics of productive and unproductive sessions. Consider the following questions:

➤ Did you understand the purpose of the session?

➤ Did everyone have an opportunity to express their opinion or ask questions?

➤ Did participants feel pressured to express their opinions?

➤ How were decisions made? Did everyone understand the process?

➤ Did the session start and end on time?

➤ Did one or two people dominate the meeting?

➤ Did everyone understand and follow through on their responsibilities/assignments?

➤ Did the discussion stay on track?

Activity 2: Practicing Public Speaking

Select any topic about which you feel very knowledgeable—whether it's a recipe, a TV show, a sport, gardening, or some aspect of child care or child development. Prepare a five-minute talk about the topic, and share it with a partner. Give each other feedback about what was easy to understand, what was unclear, etc. Work on revising your presentation, and repeat with the same partner. Consider sharing your talk with a larger group. You might also introduce this activity to your protégé.

Bellm, D. and Whitebook, M. (in press). *Leadership Empowerment Action Project (LEAP): A Training Guide for the Early Childhood Community.* Washington, DC: Center for the Child Care Workforce.

Carter, M. and Curtis, D. (1994). *Training Teachers: A Harvest of Theory and Practice.* St. Paul, MN: Redleaf Press.

Newton, A., Bergstrom, K., Brennan, N., Dunne, K., Gilbert, C., Ibarguen, N., Perez-Selles, M., and Thomas, E. (1994). *Mentoring: A Resource and Training Guide for Educators.* Andover, MA: The Regional Laboratory for Educational Improvement.

Like working with children, working with adults is a continual learning process. *The Early Childhood Mentoring Curriculum* has been designed as a beginning course, with the understanding that as a mentor, you will benefit from ongoing mentoring yourself in order to become better and better at the job as time goes on—either in an ongoing mentor support group, or by receiving continuing training.

We hope that this Curriculum has been a useful starting place for your mentoring career, and that it will be a resource to which you can turn again and again over the course of your professional development.

APPENDIX I

TEACHERS' DEVELOPMENTAL STAGES

by Lilian Katz

Teachers can generally be counted on to talk about developmental needs and stages when they discuss children. It may be equally meaningful to think of teachers themselves as having developmental sequences in their professional growth patterns (Katz and Weir, 1969). The purpose of the present discussion is to outline the tasks and associated training needs of each suggested developmental stage and to consider the implications for the timing and location of training efforts.

It seems reasonable to suggest that there may be at least four developmental stages for teachers. Individual teachers may vary greatly in the length of time spent in each of the four stages outlined below and schematized in Figure 1.

Stage I—Survival

Developmental Tasks

During this stage, which may last throughout the first full year of teaching, the teacher's main concern is whether or not she can survive. This preoccupation with survival may be expressed in terms like these: "Can I get through the day in one piece? Without losing a child? Can I make it until the end of the week—the next vacation? Can I really do this kind of work day after day? Will I be accepted by my colleagues?" Such questions are well expressed in Ryan's (1970) enlightening collection of accounts of first-year teaching experiences.

The first full impact of responsibility for a group of immature but vigorous young children (to say nothing of encounters with their parents) inevitably provokes teacher anxieties. The discrepancy between anticipated successes and classroom realities intensifies feelings of inadequacy and unpreparedness.

Training Needs

During this period the teacher needs support, understanding, encouragement, reassurance, comfort and guidance. She needs instruction in specific skills and insight into the complex causes of behavior— all of which must be provided at the classroom site. On-site trainers may be senior staff members, advisers, consultants or program assistants. Training must be constantly and readily available from someone who knows both the trainee and her teaching situation well. The trainer should have enough time and flexibility to be on call as needed by the trainee. Schedules of periodic visits which have been arranged in advance cannot be counted on to coincide with trainees' crises. Cook and Mack (1971) describe the British pattern of on-site training given to teachers by their headmasters (principals). Armington (1969) also describes the way advisers can meet these teacher needs.

Stage II—Consolidation

Developmental Tasks

By the end of the first year the teacher has usually decided that she is capable of surviving. She is now ready to consolidate the overall gains made during the first stage and to differentiate specific tasks and skills to be mastered next. During Stage II, teachers usually begin to focus on individual problem children and problem situations. This focus may take the form of looking for answers to such questions as: "How can I help a clinging child? How can I help a particular child who does not seem to be learning?"

During Stage I, the neophyte acquires a baseline of information about what young children are like and what to expect of them. By Stage II the teacher is beginning to identify individual children whose behavior departs from the pattern of most of the children she knows.

Training Needs

During this stage, on-site training continues to be valuable. A trainer can help the teacher through mutual exploration of a problem. Take, for example, the case of a young teacher from a day care center who was eager to get help and expressed her problem in the question, "How should I deal with a clinging child?" An on-site trainer can, of course, observe the teacher and child *in situ* and arrive at suggestions and tentative solution strategies fairly quickly. However, without firsthand knowledge of the child and

context, an extended give-and-take conversation between teacher and trainer may be the best way for the trainer to help the teacher to interpret her experience and move toward a solution of the problem. The trainer might ask the teacher such questions as, "What have you done so far? Give an example of some experiences with this particular child during this week. When you did such and such, how did the child respond?"

Also, in this stage the need for information about specific children suggests that learning to use a wider range of resources is needed. Psychologists, social and health workers, and other specialists can strengthen the teacher's skills and knowledge at this time. Exchanges of information and ideas with more experienced colleagues may help teachers master the developmental tasks of this period. Opportunities to share feelings with other teachers in the same stage of development may help to reduce some of the teacher's sense of personal inadequacy and frustration.

Stage III—Renewal

Developmental Tasks

Often, during the third or fourth year of teaching, the teacher begins to tire of doing the same old things. She starts to ask more questions about new developments in the field: "Who is doing what? Where? What are some of the new materials, techniques, approaches, and ideas?" It may be that what the teacher has been doing for each annual crop of children has been quite adequate for them, but that she herself finds the recurrent Valentine cards, Easter bunnies, and pumpkin cutouts insufficiently interesting. If it is true that a teacher's own interest or commitment to the projects and activities she provides for children contributes to their educational value, then her need for renewal and refreshment should be taken seriously.

Training Needs

During this stage, teachers find it especially rewarding to meet colleagues from different programs on both formal and informal occasions. Teachers in this developmental stage are particularly receptive to experiences in regional and national conferences and workshops, and profit from membership in professional associations and participation in their meetings. Teachers are now widening the scope of their reading, scanning numerous magazines and journals, and viewing films. Perhaps during this period they may be ready to take a close look at their own classroom teaching through videotaping. This is also a time when teachers welcome opportunities to visit other classes, programs and demonstration projects.

Perhaps it is at this stage that the teacher center has the greatest potential value (Silberman, 1971; Bailey, 1971). Teacher centers are places where teachers can gather together to help each other learn or relearn skills, techniques and methods, to exchange ideas, and to organize special workshops. From time to time specialists in curriculum, child growth, or any other area of concern which teachers identify are invited to the center to meet with teachers.

Stage IV—Maturity

Developmental Tasks

Maturity may be reached by some teachers within three years; in others, in five or more. The teacher at this stage has come to terms with herself as a teacher. She now has enough perspective to begin to ask deeper and more abstract questions, such as: "What are my historical and philosophical roots? What is the nature of growth and learning? How are educational decisions made? Can schools change societies? Is teaching a profession?" Perhaps she has asked these questions before. But with the experience she has now gained, the questions represent a more meaningful search for insight, perspective and realism.

Training Needs

Throughout maturity, teachers need an opportunity to participate in conferences and seminars and perhaps to work toward a degree. Mature teachers welcome the chance to read widely and to interact with educators working on many problem areas on many different levels. Training sessions and conference events which Stage II teachers enjoy may be very tiresome to the Stage IV teacher. (Similarly, introspective and searching discussion seminars enjoyed by Stage IV teachers may lead to restlessness and irritability among the beginners of Stage I.)

Summary

Four dimensions of training for teaching have been suggested: (1) developmental stages of the teacher; (2) training needs of each stage; (3) location of the training; and (4) timing of training.

1. *Developmental Stages of the Teacher*. It is useful to think of the growth of teachers as occurring in stages that are linked very generally to experience gained over time.

2. *Training Needs of Each Stage*. The training needs of teachers change as experience occurs. For example, the issues dealt with in the traditional social foundations courses do not seem to address themselves to the early survival problems which are critical to the inexperienced. However, for the maturing teacher, those same issues may help to deepen her understanding of the total complex context in which she is trying to be effective.

3. *Location of Training*. The location of training should be moved as the teacher develops. At the beginning of the new teacher's career, training resources must be taken to her so that training can be responsive to the particular (and possibly unique) developmental tasks and working situation the trainee faces in her classroom. Later on as the teacher moves past the survival stage, training can move toward the college campus.

4. *Timing of Training*. The timing of training should be shifted so that more training is available to the teacher on the job than before it. Many teachers say that their preservice education has had only a minor influence on what they do day-to-day in their classrooms, which suggests that strategies acquired before employment will often not be retrieved under pressure of concurrent forces and factors in the actual job situation.

However, even though it is often said that experience is the best teacher, we cannot assume that experience teaches what the new trainee should learn. To direct this learning, to try to make sure that the beginning teacher has informed and interpreted experience, should be one of the major roles of the teacher trainer.

Figure 1. Stages of Development and Training Needs of Preschool Teachers

Developmental Stages	Training Needs
Stage IV Maturity	⟶ Seminars, institutes, course degree programs, books, journals, conferences
Stage III Renewal	⟶ Conferences, professional associations, journals, magazines, films, visits to demonstration projects
Stage II Consolidation	⟶ On-site assistance, access to specialists, colleague advice, consultants
Stage I Survival	⟶ On-site support and technical assistance
	0 1 yr 2 yrs 3 yrs 4 yrs 5 yrs

Sources:

Armington, D., "A Plan for Continuing Growth." Mimeographed. Newton, MA: Educational Development Center, 1969. Ed 046 493.

Bailey, S.K., "Teachers' Centers: A British First," *Phi Delta Kappan* 53, No. 3 (November 1971): 146-149.

Cook, A., and Mack, M., *The Headteacher's Role*. New York: Citation Press, 1971.

Katz, L.G., and Weir, M.K., "Help for Preschool Teachers: A Proposal." Mimeographed. Urbana, IL: ERIC Clearinghouse on Early Childhood Education, 1969. Ed 031 308.

Ryan, K. ed. *Don't Smile Until Christmas: Accounts of the First Year of Teaching*. Chicago: Univ. of Chicago Press, 1970.

Silberman, A., "A Santa's Workshop for Teachers." *American Education* 7, No. 10 (1971): 3-8.

Originally published as "Developmental Stages of Preschool Teachers," by Lilian Katz, in *The Elementary School Journal* 23, No. 1 (1972): 50-51.

APPENDIX 2
CHECKLIST FOR HEALTH AND SAFETY CONDITIONS
IN CHILD CARE PROGRAMS

☛ **Use this preliminary checklist to identify major problems areas in a child care program.**

Illness/Infection

1. In the past year, have you been exposed to and/or contracted the following?:
   head lice _____ flu _____ colds _____ sore throat _____ impetigo _____
   childhood illnesses _____ hepatitis _____ giardiasis _____.

2. In the past year, have you worked when sick? _____

3. Do you have an adequate and effective substitute policy? _____

4. Is there an established policy for caring for sick children? _____.
   Is it always enforced? _____

5. Is there a separate area set aside for sick children? _____

6. How and where are children diapered?

7. How is the diapering area cleaned?

8. Have you been screened for rubella? _____ For TB? _____

Body Strains

1. In the past year, have you suffered from back, neck, shoulder or leg strains? _____

2. Is there adult-sized furniture available? _____

3. How often do you move heavy equipment or furniture? _____

4. Is there adequate and easily accessible storage available? _____

Chemicals and Art Materials

1. Name the chemicals/cleansers used in the program.

2. Are all chemicals/cleansers labeled properly with directions for use? _____
   with warnings? _____ with instructions for emergencies? _____

3. Do you use: powdered tempera? _____ permanent markers? _____ dry clay? _____
   lead glazes? _____ instant paper mache? _____ others_____?

4. Have you experienced skin, nose, eye or respiratory problems from cleaning solutions
   and/or art materials? _____

5. Do you spray with pesticides to control fleas, roaches or other vermin? _____

Stress

1. Do you feel your job is stressful? _____

2. What areas do you think are most stressful?

3. Have you experienced: headaches? _____ trouble sleeping? _____
   muscle strain? _____ eyestrain? _____ changes in menstrual cycle? _____
   digestive/stomach problems? _____ nausea/dizziness? _____ exhaustion? _____

4. Are there established, effective policies for breaks? _____ pregnant workers? _____
   grievance resolution? _____

Source: "Warning: Child Care Work May Be Hazardous to Your Health," by Marcy Whitebook, Gerri Ginsburg and Dan Bellm. *Day Care and Early Education*, Winter 1984, updated 1995.

APPENDIX 3

SELECTED READINGS ABOUT EARLY CARE AND EDUCATION IN THE UNITED STATES

Bellm, D. *Breaking the Link. A National Forum on Child Care Compensation.* Washington, DC: Center for the Child Care Workforce, 1994. Identifies problems in the current financing of child care jobs and services, and successful initiatives to raise child care salaries. Explores strategies for challenging social attitudes, developing innovative funding and financing options, and building coalitions to boost child care compensation and quality.

Carnegie Corporation of New York. *Starting Points: Meeting the Needs of Our Youngest Children.* New York: Carnegie Corporation, 1994. Discusses the major problems facing children under the age of three and their families, including poverty, inadequate health care services, child abuse, and poor-quality child care. Explores the impact of these problems on children's brain and social development, and identifies an agenda for change.

Cost, Quality and Child Outcomes Team. *Cost, Quality and Child Outcomes in Child Care Centers: Executive Summary.* Denver, CO: Economics Department, University of Colorado, 1995. A comprehensive study of center-based child care in four states, identifying elements of quality and their relationship to differences in financing. Also explores the impact of the quality of care on children's development.

Gomby, D., ed. (1996). *Financing Child Care. The Future of Children,* 6(2). Los Altos, CA: David and Lucile Packard Foundation. A comprehensive overview of funding and financing issues facing the U.S. child care delivery system today.

Johnson, J. and McCracken, J.B., eds. *The Early Childhood Career Lattice: Perspectives on Professional Development.* Washington, DC: National Association for the Education of Young Children, 1994. Explores various pathways and strategies to achieve professional development, and identifies a core curriculum for practitioners working with young children.

Kontos, S., Howes, C., Shinn, M. and Galinsky, E. *Quality in Family Child Care and Relative Care*. New York: Teachers College Press, 1995. Explores the results and implications of a national in-depth observational study of family child care and relative care, and offers a list of recommendations for upgrading the quality of care.

Morgan, G., Azer, S., Costley, J., Genser, A., Goodman, I., Lombardi, J. and McGimsey, B. *Making A Career of It: The State of the States Report on Career Development in Early Care and Education*. Boston, MA: The Center for Career Development in Early Care and Education at Wheelock College, 1993. Details the policies that determine the qualifications required, and training available, for teachers and providers in the preschool and school-age child care fields. Identifies the limitations and shortcomings of current training systems, and makes recommendations to improve the regulation, funding and delivery of training for child care practitioners.

Whitebook, M., Howes, C., and Phillips, D. *Who Cares? Child Care Teachers and the Quality of Care in America: The National Child Care Staffing Study, Final Report*. Washington, DC: Center for the Child Care Workforce, 1990. *The National Child Care Staffing Study Revisited: Four Years in the Life of Center-based Child Care*. Washington, DC: Center for the Child Care Workforce, 1993. A comprehensive profile of center-based child care teaching staff in the United States, and the impact of the adult work environment on the quality of care which children receive. The update assesses changes in wages, benefits and staff turnover during the intervening years.

APPENDIX 4
THE NATIONAL CHILD CARE STAFFING STUDY:
HIGHLIGHTS OF MAJOR FINDINGS

The National Child Care Staffing Study, conducted in 1988 and published in 1990, explored how teaching staff and their working conditions affect the caliber of center-based child care available in the United States. "Teaching staff" includes all staff who provide direct care to children. Following are highlights of the study's findings:

* *The education of child care teaching staff and the arrangement of their work environment are essential determinants of the quality of services children receive.*

Teaching staff provided more sensitive and appropriate caregiving if they completed more years of formal education, received early childhood training at the college level, earned higher wages and better benefits, and worked in centers devoting a higher percentage of the operating budget to teaching personnel.

* *The most important predictor of the quality of care which children receive, among all the variables in adult work environments, is staff wages.*

The quality of services provided by most centers was rated as barely adequate. Better-quality centers had:

- → higher wages,
- → better adult work environments,
- → lower teaching staff turnover,
- → better educated and trained staff, and
- → more teachers caring for fewer children.

Better-quality centers were more likely to be operated on a nonprofit basis, to be accredited by the National Association for the Education of Young Children, to be located in states with higher standards of quality, and to meet adult-child ratio, group size and staff training provisions contained in the 1980 Federal Interagency Day Care Requirements.

* *Despite having higher levels of formal education than the average American worker, child care teaching staff earn abysmally low wages.*

In 1988, this predominately female work force earned an average hourly wage of $5.35. In the previous decade, child care staff wages, when adjusted for inflation, had decreased more than 20%.

Child care teaching staff earn less than half as much as comparably educated women, and less than one-third as much as comparably educated men in the civilian labor force.

* *Staff turnover has nearly tripled during the previous decade, jumping from 15% in 1977 to 41% in 1988.*

The most important determinant of staff turnover, among all the variable in adult work environments, was staff wages.

Teaching staff earning the lowest wages were twice as likely to leave their jobs as those earning the highest wages.

* *Children attending lower-quality centers and centers with more staff turnover are less competent in language and social development.*

* *Children of low- and high-income families are more likely than children of middle-income families to attend centers providing higher-quality care.*

* *Compared with a decade before, child care centers in the United States receive fewer governmental funds, are more likely to be operated on a for-profit basis, and care for a larger number of infants.*

1992 UPDATE

In 1992, National Child Care Staffing Study researchers conducted an update of the 1988 study, and found that only 85% of the 227 centers that had participated in the original study remained open. Their directors, 60% of whom were the same as in 1988, participated in telephone interviews to provide a revised portrait of typical center-based care. We found that:

* *Teaching staff continue to earn exceptionally low wages compared to other, often less educated and trained members of the civilian labor force.*

Real wages for the lowest-paid teaching assistants, the fastest growing segment of the child care work force, declined since 1988 to $5.08 an hour. This translates to an annual salary of $8,890 per year.

Real wages for the highest-paid teaching staff, who constitute a very small segment of the work force, improved only modestly, approximately 66 cents an hour over four years. This translates to an annual salary of $15,488 per year.

- *Despite teachers' heavy exposure to illness on the job, the overwhelming majority of centers offer their teaching staff no or limited health insurance.*

  Only 27% of centers provided fully-paid health insurance for their teaching staff, and of these, 32% did not cover assistant teachers.

- *Turnover of teaching staff continues to be high, threatening the ability of centers to offer consistent services to children.*

Between 1988 and 1992, 70% of the teaching staff interviewed in 1988 had left their jobs. Those earning $5.00 per hour or less in 1988 left at a rate of 77%, compared to a 53% turnover rate for teaching staff earning over $7.00 per hour.

Turnover between 1991 and 1992 dropped to 26%, but still remained close to three times the annual turnover of 9.6% reported by all U.S. companies, and well above the 5.6% turnover rate reported for public school teachers.

Excerpted from *The National Child Care Staffing Study: Who Cares? Child Care Teachers and the Quality of Care in America*, Washington, DC: Center for the Child Care Workforce, 1990, and the *National Child Care Staffing Study Revisited: Four Years in the Life of Center-based Child Care*, Washington, DC: Center for the Child Care Workforce, 1993.

APPENDIX 5
CHILD CARE WORK FORCE FACTS

There are an estimated three million child care teachers, teaching assistants and family child care providers in the United States. They care for 10 million children each day.

97% OF ALL TEACHING STAFF ARE FEMALE
33% OF ALL TEACHING STAFF ARE WOMEN OF COLOR
41% OF ALL TEACHING STAFF HAVE CHILDREN
10% OF ALL TEACHING STAFF ARE SINGLE PARENTS

➤ Child care teaching staff earn an average of $6.70 per hour, or $11,725 per year (based on a 35-hour week/52-week year).[1]

➤ Only 18% of child care centers offer health coverage to teaching staff. The average rate of health coverage is much higher nationally. It is estimated that 85% of Americans receive health coverage from some source.

➤ Men in the U.S. earn an average of $30,407 per year, almost three times as much as child care staff. Women in the civilian labor force, at an average of $21,747 per year, earn twice as much as child care teaching staff.[2]

➤ Although they earn substantially lower wages, child care teachers are better educated than the general population.

➤ One-third of all child care teachers leave their centers each year.

---

[1] *National Child Care Staffing Study Revisited* (1993). Salary data in 1994 dollars.

[2] U.S. Department of Labor, Bureau of Labor Statistics.

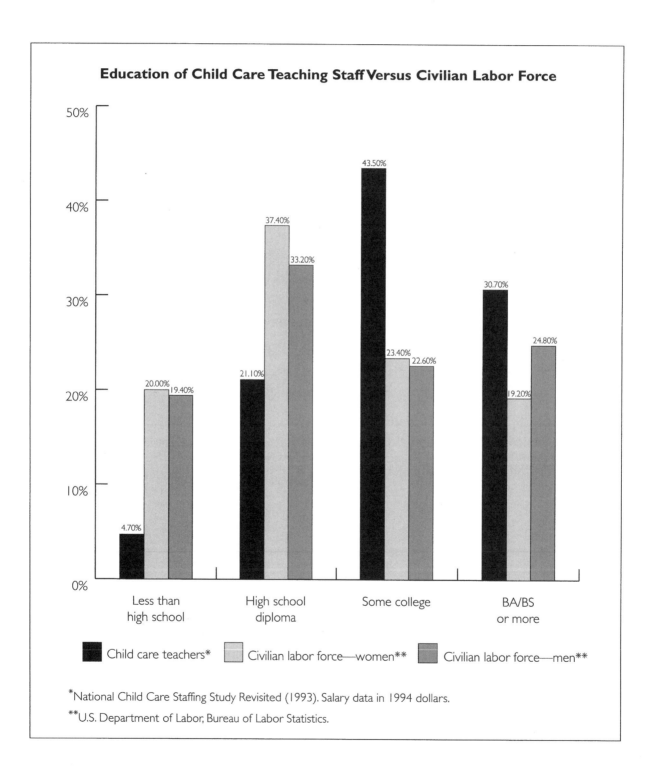

Education of Child Care Teaching Staff Versus Civilian Labor Force

	Less than high school	High school diploma	Some college	BA/BS or more
Child care teachers*	4.70%	21.10%	43.50%	30.70%
Civilian labor force—women**	20.00%	37.40%	23.40%	19.20%
Civilian labor force—men**	19.40%	33.20%	22.60%	24.80%

■ Child care teachers*   ▨ Civilian labor force—women**   ▨ Civilian labor force—men**

*National Child Care Staffing Study Revisited (1993). Salary data in 1994 dollars.

**U.S. Department of Labor, Bureau of Labor Statistics.

An experienced teacher describes the way low wages affects her center:

> *"I started as head teacher six years ago and I'm still here....I train all new employees and bring new ideas and changes to current employees. I am getting twenty cents per hour more because of this. Even with this raise and years of service, I still only make $5.80 per hour. How sad! Sadness is when two young teachers who have been with us for a year both left our day care center to work at Taco Bell. Their starting pay was ten cents an hour more than they made here. The benefits at Taco Bell were better too."*[3]

How child care center teachers tell us they support themselves and their families on their wages:

THEY HOLD SECOND JOBS
THEY LIVE WITH THEIR PARENTS
THEY DEPEND ON A SECOND INCOME
THEY FORGO HEALTH INSURANCE AND MEDICAL CARE

When child care center teachers can't live on low wages any longer, they leave their jobs, thus jeopardizing the quality of care for millions of children each year.

> *Family child care providers who care for and educate young children in their homes also have very low earnings. Regulated providers earned $15,649 before expenses and nonregulated providers earned just $8,026 in 1993.[4] After expenses, regulated providers earned an estimated $8,627, and nonregulated providers earned $4,114.*

---

[3] *Valuable Work, Minimal Rewards* (1994). Center for the Child Care Workforce.

[4] *The Study of Children in Family Child Care and Relative Care* (1994). Families and Work Institute.

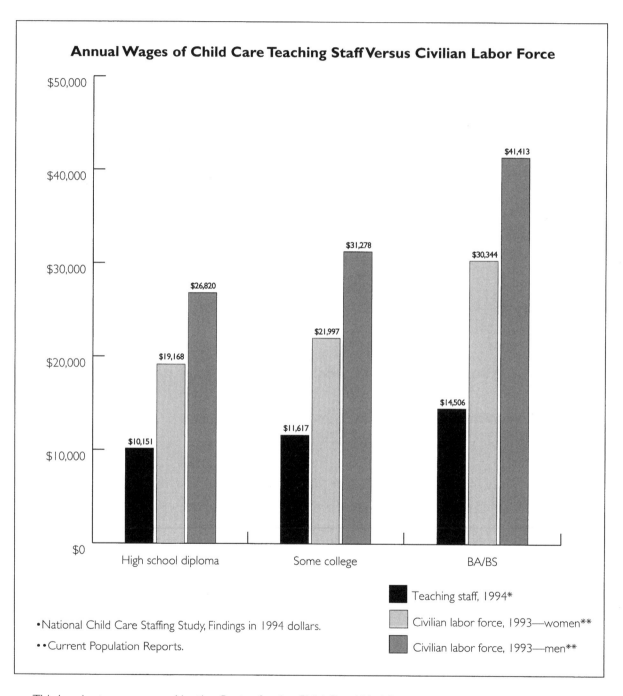

Annual Wages of Child Care Teaching Staff Versus Civilian Labor Force

	High school diploma	Some college	BA/BS
Teaching staff, 1994*	$10,151	$11,617	$14,506
Civilian labor force, 1993—women**	$19,168	$21,997	$30,344
Civilian labor force, 1993—men**	$26,820	$31,278	$41,413

■ Teaching staff, 1994*

▨ Civilian labor force, 1993—women**

▨ Civilian labor force, 1993—men**

•National Child Care Staffing Study, Findings in 1994 dollars.

••Current Population Reports.

This handout was prepared by the Center for the Child Care Workforce.

APPENDIX 6
MENTOR QUESTIONNAIRE

We would like to gather some information from you that will help us improve the mentoring program. Your individual responses will remain confidential. A compilation of all mentors' responses will be shared with you and your colleagues.

Please read each question carefully. Respond by checking "yes" or "no," or by writing your answer in the space provided. Return your completed questionnaire to:

_____

My role as a mentor and the support I received from others:

1. How long have you been a mentor? _____ months

2. What individuals, activities or readings were most helpful in enabling you to understand your role as a mentor?
   Individuals:_____
   Activities:_____
   Readings:_____

3. What other activities might assist you in gaining this understanding?

   _____
   _____
   _____
   _____

4. What kinds of support were most valuable in helping you to fulfill your role?

   _____
   _____
   _____
   _____

5. What kinds of support were less helpful?

_____

_____

_____

_____

6. How many times did you observe your protégé in a typical month? _____ times

7. How many times did your protégé observe you in a typical month? _____ times

8. To your knowledge, how many times did your protégé observe other teachers or providers working with children in a typical month? _____ times

9. Did you and your protégé meet at (please check all that apply):
   ❑   a specified time each week
   ❑   other (please specify) _____

10. Please describe any strategies you employed to find time to meet with your protégé.

_____

_____

_____

_____

11. Please describe any strategies you believe the mentoring program should employ to facilitate finding time with your protégé.

_____

_____

_____

_____

12. Please describe any strategies you used that were effective in building a collegial relationship with your protégé.

_____
_____
_____
_____

Interest in serving as a mentor in the future:

1. Would you be willing to be a mentor again?
   ❑   yes
   ❑   no

If yes, why would you be willing to serve again?

_____
_____
_____

If no, what would keep you from serving as a mentor again?

_____
_____
_____

Open-ended questions:

1. One real benefit of being a mentor was . . .

_____
_____
_____
_____

2. The biggest challenge that I had this year as a mentor was . . .

_____

_____

_____

_____

3. As a mentor, I wish I had known . . .

_____

_____

_____

_____

4. If I were to give advice to a new mentor, it would be . . .

_____

_____

_____

_____

5. The most important thing I learned from my protégé was . . .

_____

_____

_____

_____

6. If I were to design a mentor training program, I would emphasize . . .

_____

_____

_____

_____

Thank your for your assistance.

Source: Adapted with permission of the author from "Mentor Questionnaire," by Elaine Holt, Nashua Public Schools, Nashua, NH.

APPENDIX 7
PROTÉGÉ QUESTIONNAIRE

We would like to gather some information from you that will help us improve the mentoring program. Your individual responses will remain confidential. A compilation of all responses will be shared with you and your colleagues.

Please read each question carefully. Respond by checking "yes" or "no," or by writing your answer in the space provided. Return your completed questionnaire to:

_____

My experience as a protégé:

1. Did you and your mentor find time to meet?

   ❑   yes

   ❑   no

If yes, how did you manage this?

_____
_____
_____
_____

2. In a typical month, how many times did you meet with your mentor? _____ times

3. Did you meet at (please check all that apply):

   ❑   a specified time each week

   ❑   other (please specify) _____

_____

4. How many times did you observe your mentor in a typical month? _____ times

5. How many times did you observe other teachers or providers in a typical month? _____ times

6. How many times did your mentor observe you in a typical month? _____ times

7. Did you discuss these observations? If yes, how did you find the time?

_____

_____

_____

_____

Open-ended questions:

1. The biggest challenge that I had this year was . . .

_____

_____

_____

_____

2. At the beginning of the year, I wish I had known . . .

_____

_____

_____

_____

3. One benefit of having a mentor was . . .

_____

_____

_____

_____

4. The most important thing I learned from my mentor was . . .

_____

_____

_____

_____

5. If I were a mentor and I had a protégé, I would be sure to . . .

_____

_____

_____

_____

6. If I were to design a mentor training program, I would emphasize . . .

_____

_____

_____

_____

Thank you for your assistance.

Source: Adapted with permission of the author from "New Teacher Questionnaire," by Elaine Holt, Nashua Public Schools, Nashua, NH.